A TASTING OF
ALAN KINSELLA
AT LOCKS RESTAURANT

12 Tasting Menus created by
International Chef
Alan Kinsella

ashfield
PRESS

First published in 2005 by
ASHFIELD PRESS•DUBLIN•IRELAND

ISBN: 1 901658 48 1

Typeset by Ashfield Press in 12 on 14.5 point Dante and Frutiger

Designed by
SUSAN WAINE

Photography
ALAN KINSELLA

Printed in Ireland by
BETAPRINT LIMITED, DUBLIN

A TASTING OF
ALAN KINSELLA

AT LOCKS RESTAURANT

Pour
Eric mon
frère d'Arlamele
Cousinement

Contents

How to use this book

IMPORTANT NOTE ON RECIPES

All the recipes in the menu are in small portion sizes, some for four and some for eight. Some of the portions may look large if you are having eight courses, but it is better to have too much than to too little. Remember that not everybody will like everything. You can please some of the people some of the time but not all of them all of the time. If you should decide not to opt for a tasting menu, with all its associated courses, simply double the ingredients for a standard-sized course.

The recipes vary because some of them need to be made in large quantities to be worth making. Feel free to divide or multiply the recipe. It will work either way.

The dessert recipes are for large portions as I thought that the sweet tooth would appreciate that.

Any terms or ingredients not understood are explained in the Glossory on page 163.

OVEN TEMPERATURE CONVERSION CHART

Gas Mark 1	275°F	140°C
2	330°F	150°C
3	325°F	170°C
4	350°F	180°C
5	375°F	190°C
6	400°F	200°C
7	425°F	220°C
8	450°F	230°C
9	475°F	240°C

To my son Michael, my love for you is forever boundless.

Food is created by the desire for change in traditions, produce and maturing tastes in people.
Chefs are created by changing to maturing tastes and creating new traditions.

ALAN KINSELLA

Introduction by Alan Kinsella

In 1987, I finished school. I was just 17 and had no idea what I wanted to do. That September, a teacher from my school opened a restaurant and gave me my first job. He sacked me on Christmas Eve and told me to find a new career. I can't say that I shed many tears when the restaurant closed just three months later.

My next job was in a local burger bar and lasted four months. Then I started a 13-week chef's course during which I was picked to go on a pilot course to Spain on a scholarship for 13 weeks. What a holiday – I learnt very little but had a great time!

On my return, I started at the CERT College at Rosslare for six months, which was followed by placements at a number of hotels and restaurants, as well as further study. I was close to giving it all up but was then awarded another scholarship, this time to attend a one-year diploma course in Belgium. While the course wasn't wonderful, it did involve working in a Michelin two-star restaurant, and so began my love with the food and standards associated with Michelin restaurants.

After Belgium, I moved on to four more countries over the next three years, always working in Michelin 1 or 2-star restaurants.

Then I met my wife. We went to Australia for six years where I worked and ran fine dining restaurants, winning three awards. Our son Michael was born in 1999 and three years later we decided to return to Ireland. I started in Locks restaurant in July of 2003.

MY PASSION

My principle passion in cooking is to achieve to a high standard of cuisine so that I can earn a Michelin star or two of my own.

MY INFLUENCES

Marco Pierre White's was the only cookbook that I had as a chef. His passion and food influenced me to the point that I thought of nothing but how to cook and become him. With age came maturity and wisdom. Now I want to be myself and to be a chef who maintains high standards and is known for doing so.

TO OTHER CHEFS

If you really have the passion to become a good chef, then do whatever it takes to become one. The long hours, the screaming head chefs, the stress and no social life - remember, these are the good things and not the negatives of being a chef!

One day, having gone to hell and back 50 times a day for the last five years, you will reflect and see that it was all worth it, that you would not trade it for anything or anyone. Trust me, I have the scars, both mental and physical, to prove it. But where I am today I would not change for anything.

ABOUT THIS BOOK

The ideas and recipes in this book are those I have used over the last year at Locks restaurant. I have put together some ideas that go well together but each dish can be changed to your own personal liking. That's the beauty of taste buds, everybody's are different. The recipes are small for tasting menu courses. How big or small is up to you. I have also used the same product or recipe over and over again to illustrate how most things will go well with other things. It's up to you.

At Locks, we do a surprise tasting menu every Wednesday in the restaurant. The success of these nights has inspired me to write this tasting menu cookbook.

Foreword by Claire Douglas

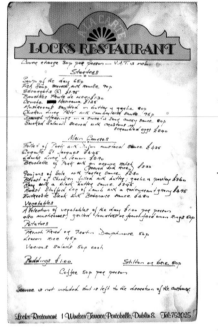

Locks first ever menu

LOCKS RESTAURANT was born out of our passion for good food, whether it was a simple meal from a bodega in Mexico, a Michelin three-star restaurant gourmands heaven in Paris, or simply a marvellous old recipe found and experimented with at home.

At the time we first thought of opening a restaurant, Richard was an international banker and I was the London correspondent for a Danish newspaper. Richard was Irish and our frequent visits back to Dublin persuaded us that Dublin was the right place to open. I had taken a course in hotel management years before and Richard gave up his job and took a catering course. After he had worked in a few restaurants, we decided the time had come to take the plunge.

We arrived in Dublin in 1979 and after an exhaustive search finally found a dilapidated corner shop with a garage on the banks of the leafy Grand Canal in Portobello that seemed to fit what we were looking for - in spite of the fact that Richard's father, a consultant at the Meath Hospital just down the road, said that he would never be seen eating lunch in Portobello.

After begging for loans and a lot of hard work, the restaurant finally opened in August 1980 and we named it Locks after the locks on the canal. And a marvellous opening party later, we were a huge success.

I had grown up with Paris as my second home and had dreamt of opening a Brasserie in Dublin. While we were doing up Locks, I happened upon Prior interiors in Dawson Street, which had the most wonderful old ballroom and a feeling of space that reminded me of my favourite brasserie in Paris, La Coupole. When the lease came up we jumped at it and created the first proper brasserie in Dublin, Café Klara named after our daughter Klara. Unfortunately, several years later, Richard and I separated, and Café Klara was sold, becoming what is now La Stampa. Richard went on to found the Douglas Food Co., which became a Dublin institution and provided meals and dinner parties for those too busy to cook themselves. He later sold Douglas Food Co. and was planning on retiring to Spain where he sadly passed away in 2000.

I carried on running Locks, which, with its white panelling and timeless atmosphere, has always attracted people from all walks of life. Many famous people have dined at Locks over the years and the restaurant has always been known for the discretion and

professionalism of its staff, one of whom, Liam Farrell has worked in the restaurant for 21 years.

In the early days, many of the recipes were adapted from my grandmother's old recipes, such as black pudding with a duck fat and onion sauce which became famous, herrings in a curry sauce and pigs heart stuffed with prunes.

We have had several talented chefs over the years. Our first head chef, Kevin McCarthy created a Jugged Hare that still makes my mouth water to this day. Another was Brian Buckley, who created another of our popular dishes, crispy potato skins stuffed with prawns, smoked salmon, spinach and tomato, all cooked in cream and glazed with hollandaise sauce, for which we still get requests today. Noel Cusack was sous chef in Locks when he created a wonderful smoked haddock dish, before he went on to become head chef in Café Klara.

Our son Jamie is now involved in the business and helps with the day-to-day running, in particular taking a great interest in the wines. Our other two children, Kristian and Klara, help out at the holidays and we all share a certain gastronomic precociousness.

Alan Kinsella arrived in Locks two years ago and we decided to scrap the old dishes and thrust Locks into the 21st century, a decision which has been greeted warmly by our old customers as well as being applauded by many new ones, although more than few tears were shed over the previously mentioned dishes. We believe Alan is a great Chef and will let this book and our restaurant speak for themselves.

We wish to thank all those who have supported us over the last twenty-five years, both customers and suppliers, and look forward to our half century.

Roasted Pigeon Breast, Stuffed Pigeon Leg and Pomme Anna (*page 17*)

Duck Rillette with Foie Gras and Baileys cream sauce

INGREDIENTS (SERVES 4)

1	duck large, about 1kg
120g	foie gras
80ml	Baileys cream sauce
30g	frisée lettuce
10g	mustard cress

METHOD

1. Confit the duck by covering the duck in oil (or duck fat if you have it) and cooking on a very gentle heat, about 50°C for about three hours. Remove all the meat from the bones while still hot. Rub and shred the meat through your fingers and season.
2. Allow the confit fat to set, then separate the fat from the jelly beneath.
3. Add 10g fat and 10g jelly to every 100g of meat. Roll tightly into a sausage shape of about 1cm in diameter in cling film and place in the fridge to set. This is called a rillette. From one large duck you should get about 250g of meat off the bone.
4. Take the set rillette and cut into 8 slices.
5. The foie gras for this recipe is poached and should give you four slices. Alternatively, you can just cut into four slices and panfry them on a smoking hot pan for 10 seconds each side. *(see p. 59)*

(see p. 59)

TO SERVE

1. Mix the lettuce and the cress together with your favourite dressing.
2. Arrange the rillette and foie gras on the plate, dress with the salad and drizzle with Baileys cream sauce, which can be served hot or cold.

Duck Rillette with Foie Gras
and Baileys Cream Sauce

⌒⌒

Lobster Soup
and Lobster Salad

⌒⌒

Roast Pigeon Breast,
Stuffed Leg, Pomme Anna

⌒⌒

Apple Sorbet
with Apple Crisp

⌒⌒

Sole and Lobster Paupiette

⌒⌒

Stuffed Quail with
Black Pudding,
Quail Scotch Egg and
Quail Egg Salad

⌒⌒

Mature Stilton with
Red Onion Jam

⌒⌒

Hazelnut and Amaretto Parfait
with Pistachio Cream

Baileys cream sauce

INGREDIENTS

150ml cream
50ml   Baileys liqueur
3   shallots
50g   butter

METHOD

1. Sweat the shallots in the butter until soft. Add the Baileys and the cream, and reduce to a coating consistency. Season and pass.

· ·

Cream of Lobster Soup with a Lobster Salad

INGREDIENTS (SERVES 8 SMALL PORTIONS)

500g	lobster shells	20ml	brandy
1	carrot	2lt	water
1	leek	500ml	cream
100g	onion, chopped		Seasoning
100ml	white wine	100g	butter
100g	tomato trimmings	240g	lobster meat
30ml	Pernod	50g	mixed lettuce

METHOD

1. Roast the shells and vegetables on a meat tray in a hot oven then place them in a heavy pot. Deglaze the meat tray with the white wine and place in the pot.
2. Add the tomato trimmings, Pernod, brandy and the water and simmer for three hours.
3. Strain, return to a clean pot and reduce by half.
4. Add the cream and reduce by half. Season. Finish the soup by whisking in 100g of cold butter.
5. Cook the lobster in boiling water for six minutes. Remove meat and divide into four.

→

TO SERVE

1. Dress the salad with your favourite dressing and add the lobster meat. Strain the soup again and serve. Place the soup into a soup cup and garnish with the salad on the side or in a small bowl if you wish.

MY TIP

This soup can also be made by combining equal quantities of lobster fond and cream, then reducing by half. Season and pass.

· ·

Roasted Pigeon Breast, Stuffed Pigeon Leg and Pomme Anna (*see page 14*)

INGREDIENTS (SERVES 4 SMALL PORTIONS)

2	pigeons (4 breasts, 4 legs)		1	tomato, peeled and diced
2	large Rooster Potatoes		40g	cucumber, peeled, deseeded and diced
40g	grape relish (*see p. 61*)			
1tsp	white truffle oil		1tsp	Balsamic dressing (*see p. 147*)
50g	butter		30g	chicken mince
30g	frisée lettuce		1tsp	crushed pistachio nuts
10g	Lollo Rosso		1	sheet of crépinette

METHOD

1. To make the Pomme Anna (Anna Potatoes), slice the potatoes wafer thin with the mandaline. Dip the slices in melted butter and lay in a circle over lapping each other, using about 6-7 slices for each. Make 8. Place on sill mat and bake in oven at 200° C until golden brown.
2. Divide the grape relish and place on top of four of the Pomme Anna when cooked and then top with another Pomme Anna, like a sandwich. Keep warm.
3. Make a salad from the lettuce, tomato and cucumber and the balsamic dressing. Flavour with truffle oil.
4. Remove the legs from the pigeons and take out the thigh bone.

→

5. Combine the chicken meat and pistachio nuts to make a farce (stuffing), then season.
6. Stuff the legs and roll into a cylinder shape. Lay the sheet of crépinette out on work surface. Cut it into four squares of 10cm by 10cm, and wrap the legs tightly with the crépinette. Panfry gently in some oil or butter and place into a hot oven for 6 minutes.
7. Season and oil the crowns of pigeons (this is a bird with only a breast and no legs), then roast for 8 minutes at 200°C. Rest for 4 minutes and remove the breasts from the crown.

TO SERVE
1. Warm the Pomme Anna.
2. Place the pigeon breast on the centre of the plate and cut the end off the leg so it will stand. Place the leg beside the breast and the Pomme Anna on the breast. Place some of the lettuce on the Anna potato and drizzle with a dressing or a sauce of your choice.

• •

Apple Sorbet with an Apple Crisp

INGREDIENTS (SERVES 8 SMALL PORTIONS)

325g   apple purée
20g   lemon juice
250g   water
100g   sugar
75g   glucose

METHOD
1. Make the apple purée by peeling and coring the apples, then cooking at a low heat for 10 minutes with a little water until soft.
2. Bring the water, juice, sugar and glucose to the boil for 4 minutes. Add the apple purée and allow to cool. Place into an ice cream machine to finish, then place in the freezer.

MY TIP
Use already made purée. They taste just as good.

Sole and Lobster Paupiette with Paysanne of Vegetables and a Lobster Foam

INGREDIENTS (SERVES 8 SMALL PORTIONS)

480g	fillets of sole	50g	butter
240g	lobster meat, cooked (see p. 160)	100g	leeks, carrots, turnips, celeriac and courgettes, cut Paysanne-style
100ml	lobster sauce (see p. 149)		
50ml	cream		

METHOD

1. Place the fillets between two sheets of cling film and batten out slightly. Trim the ends so that they are all the same length.
2. Divide the fillets into four portions of about 4-5 pieces per portion.
3. Blend the trimmed ends of the fillets (about 80g) to a purée with the cream for about 1 minute until smooth and pass through a tamis. Add the chopped cooked lobster meat and season.
4. Place a sheet of cling film on a clean surface and lay out a portion of the fillets,

beside each other. Spread a quarter of the mousse over the fillets. Roll up tightly into a cylinder shape or paupiette. Repeat for the other three portions. Cook in simmering water for 6 minutes.

5. Cook the paysanne of vegetables separately in lightly salted boiling water and refresh.

TO SERVE

1. Warm the vegetables in the butter and place in the centre of the plate. Slice the paupiettes and place on top. Each paupiette serves two small portions.
2. Foam the lobster sauce and drizzle over the sole.

• •

Roasted Quail Stuffed with Black Pudding and Pistachio, Quail Scotch Eggs and Poached Quail Egg Salad

INGREDIENTS (SERVES 8 SMALL PORTIONS)

4	quail, boneless	1	egg
60g	pistachio nuts	100ml	milk
100g	black pudding	50g	flour
8	quail eggs	1	sheet of crépinette
150g	chicken mince meat	10ml	white wine vinegar
20g	frisée lettuce	200ml	water
20g	lambs lettuce	50ml	rosemary jus (see p. 58)
100g	breadcrumbs	10ml	Balsamic dressing (see p.147)

METHOD

1. Blend together 110g of the chicken mince and all the black pudding. Roughly chop the pistachio nuts and add to the mince. Season.
2. Stuff the quails with the mince and roll the quails so they look like there own shape again. Wrap in crépinette.
3. Place four quail eggs in boiling salted water for 3 minutes. Remove and place in iced water to refresh. Carefully peel and set aside.
4. Simmer the water in a pot, add the vinegar and poach the remaining four quail eggs carefully for 3 minutes. Remove the eggs and refresh.
5. Take the peeled quail eggs and wrap the rest of the chicken mince around them

→

carefully. Breadcrumb the eggs. This is done by first lightly flouring the eggs. Mix the (standard) egg and milk together, dip the floured eggs into this and then coat in the breadcrumbs.

6. Seal the quails and cook in the oven at 200°C for 8 minutes.
7. Deepfry the scotch eggs for 2-3 minutes until golden brown.

TO SERVE
1. Toss the lettuce in the balsamic dressing.
2. Slice the quail and cut the Scotch eggs in half. Put the poached egg on lettuce and drizzle with the warm rosemary jus.
3. Each quail will serve two portions.

MY TIP
Use quails that have been boned-out from the back so that the breasts and legs are still attached to the skin and in one piece. Ask your butcher to do this.

Mature English Stilton with Red Onion Jam and Frisée Salad

INGREDIENTS (SERVES 8 SMALL PORTIONS)

240g mature Stilton
120g red onion jam
60g frisée salad
10ml pistachio oil (*see p. 52*)

For red onion jam
200g red onions, sliced
50g white sugar
50ml red wine
50ml port wine
50g honey
50g butter

METHOD
1. Combine the sugar, wine, port, honey and butter and caramelise slightly.
2. Add the onions and reduce, stirring constantly so the bottom does not burn, till the liquid is of a honey consistency. Serve hot or cold.

TO SERVE
1. Slice the Stilton and garnish with red onion jam and frisée salad. Drizzle with the pistachio oil.

Hazelnut and Amaretto Parfait and Pistachio Cream

INGREDIENTS (SERVES 16 SMALL PORTIONS)

1lt	cream	50ml	Amaretto liqueur
140g	sugar	100g	pistachio nuts
7	egg yolks	200ml	pastry cream (*see p.147*)
100g	peeled hazelnuts		Chocolate garnishes

METHOD

1. Whip the sugar and the eggs together until they are light and fluffy.
2. Semi-whip the cream and add the Amaretto.
3. Crush the hazelnuts and add to the cream. Fold everything together gently and place in a terrine lined with cling film. Freeze.
4. To make the pistachio cream, add 100g crushed pistachio nuts to 200ml pastry cream.

TO SERVE

1. Slice the parfait and serve with pistachio cream and chocolate garnish, if required.

Tower of Crab with Mango and Orange, Frisée Lettuce and Panfried Red Mullet

INGREDIENTS (SERVES 8)

600 g	crabmeat, cooked	100	cucumber, peeled, cored and diced	
80ml	crème de cassis dressing (see p.147)	2	tomato, skinned, seeded and diced	
100g	mango, peeled and diced	30g	frisée lettuce	
100g	orange, peeled, segmented and diced	8	fillets of red mullet	
		10ml	herb oil (see p.148)	
		10ml	balsamic reduction (see p.147)	

METHOD

1. Bind the crabmeat with half the dressing.
2. Place the meat in 8 rings, each two inches in diameter, or any ring will do.
3. Divide the mango, orange, cucumber and tomato between the rings on top of crab.
4. Dress the frisée lettuce with the herb oil and place on top.
5. Remove all bones and scales from the red mullet very carefully and gently panfry them in some butter. $1^{1}/_{2}$ mins on skin side, 1 minute on other.

TO SERVE

1. Remove rings and place the towers in centre of plates.
2. Garnish with oil and balsamic reduction.
3. Place the red mullet on top of lettuce.
4. Use the remaining dressing to sauce the dish.

MY TIP

You can now buy crabmeat that has been cleaned and cooked already in good fish shops, delicatessens and supermarkets. Check it carefully to make sure there is no shell in it.

Tower of Crab with Mango and Orange, Frisée Lettuce and Panfried Red Mullet

Oxtail Consommé

Confit Duck Leg Risotto with a Truffle Jus and Parmesan Crisp

Pineapple Sorbet

Seared Ray Skate with Parmentiére Potatoes, Asparagus and Caper Vinaigrette

Ballotine of Grouse and White Pudding, with a Red Cabbage Jam and Whiskey Sauce

Goats Cheese Soufflé, Salad Bouquet and an Orange Dressing

Hot Chocolate Pudding with Chocolate Chip Ice Cream and an Orange and Berry Salad

Seared Ray 'Skate' with Parmetiere
Potatoes, Asparagus and Caper
Vinaigrette (page 28)

Oxtail Consomme with Brunoise of Vegetables and Oxtail meat

INGREDIENTS (SERVES 8)

1kg	oxtail
1lt	veal stock *(see p. 158)*
100g	chicken mince

100g	mireapoix, minced
5	egg whites
100g	brunoise of vegetables

METHOD

1. Simmer the oxtail in the stock for 2 hours until the meat is starting to fall off the bone.
2. Strain the stock. Remove the meat and reserve.
3. Shred the meat with your fingertips to use as the garnish for the soup.
4. Cool the stock so it is cold.
5. Mix together the minced vegetables, egg whites and the chicken mince.
6. Whisk this mixture into the stock and slowly bring to a boil until the 'raft floats' - the mince, whites and minced vegetables bind together and float like a raft.
7. When it comes to the boil, simmer very slowly so as not to disturb the raft.
8. Simmer for 1 hour and strain very carefully. Season.
9. The liquid should be clear and amber in colour.

TO SERVE

1. Pour into a soup bowl and garnish with the meat from the ox tail and the brunoise of vegetables. The vegetables can be raw as the hot soup will cook them.

Confit Duck Leg Risotto with a Truffle Jus and Parmesan Crisp (page 27)

INGREDIENTS (SERVES 8)

80g	brunoise of vegetables (carrots, leeks, shallot and courgettes)	50g	butter
		100ml	truffle jus
400g	cooked risotto (see p. 152)	5ml	herb oil (see p. 148)
30ml	cream (optional)	50ml	chicken stock (see p. 159)
320g	confit duck meat (see p. 153)	8	parmesan crisps (see p. 160)
			Truffle slice

METHOD

1. Sweat the carrots, leeks, shallot and courgettes in the butter until soft and add the stock. Add the risotto and toss quickly to warm. A little stock will help warm the rissoto without it becoming too sticky. If using, add the cream at this point.
2. Warm the duck meat in some herb oil and season both the risotto and meat.
3. Divide the meat between 8 rings, each of 2.5cm diameter, and flatten down. Place the risotto on top and again flatten.

Truffle jus

INGREDIENTS

30ml	white truffle oil	30g	butter
20g	truffle pieces	3	shallots, chopped
100ml	duck jus (see p.159)	50ml	red wine

MY TIP

If you would like the truffle jus to have a richer flavour, finish it with 50g cold butter, whisked in slowly until incorporated.

METHOD

1. Sweat the shallot in the butter until soft and add the wine. Reduce by half.
2. Add the oil at this stage along with the duck jus. Reduce by half, pass through sieve and season.
3. Finish with the truffle pieces.

TO SERVE

1. Place the duck confit and risotto on each plate, remove the rings.
2. Drizzle with the truffle jus and garnish with the crisp and a slice of truffle.

Confit Duck Leg Risotto with a Truffle Jus and Parmesan Crisp (page 26)

Pineapple Sorbet

INGREDIENTS (SERVES 8)

325g	pineapple purée	100g	sugar
250ml	water	75g	glucose

METHOD

1. To make the pineapple purée, peel the pineapple, cut into chunks and blend to a pulp. It can then be sieved through a tamis. It doesn't have to be cooked.
2. Bring the water, sugar and glucose to the boil for 3 minutes. Cool and add the pineapple purée. Finish in an ice cream machine until formed.

TO SERVE

1. Put one scoop of the sorbet into a glass and garnish with a pineapple crisp, if you want.

Seared Ray 'Skate' with Parmentière Potatoes, Asparagus and Caper Vinaigrette (page 24)

INGREDIENTS (SERVES 4)

4	ray / skate wings, about 150g each	80ml	vinaigrette (see p. 153)
1	large Rooster potato, about 200g	50g	butter
8	asparagus spears		Oil for Frying
		30g	capers

METHOD

1. Dice the potato into cubes of about 1cm by 1cm.
2. Blanch the asparagus in salty water for about 1 minute until al dente.
3. Panfry the skate for about 2 minutes on each side.
4. Sauté the potatoes in some butter until golden brown and crisp.
5. Warm the vinaigrette and add the capers. The asparagus can be also warmed in the vinaigrette at this stage.

TO SERVE

1. Remove the meat from the bone and place in the centre of the plate. Drizzle some vinaigrette over them.
2. Put the potatoes on top and garnish plates with warm asparagus.

....

Ballotine of Grouse and White Pudding with a Red Cabbage Jam and Whiskey Sauce

INGREDIENTS (SERVES 8)

2	whole grouse boneless like quail	50g	honey
100g	white pudding	50ml	red wine
100g	chicken mince	50ml	port wine
	crépinette	50ml	red wine vinegar
400g	red cabbage	50g	butter
50g	sugar	100ml	whiskey sauce
			(see p. 161)

METHOD

1. Lay the 2 grouse open and skin side down on some tinfoil.
2. Chop the white pudding into Brunoise-size pieces *(see p.163)*, mix with the chicken mince and season.
3. Place the mix inside the 2 grouse and roll into a cylinder shape. Wrap in crépinette and then wrap it very tightly in some tinfoil to form a smooth cylinder.
4. Roast in a preheated oven at 200°C for 20-25 minutes. Remove the foil. *This is a ballotine.*
5. Julienne the red cabbage and sweat in the butter until it starts to wilt. Add the sugar, honey and vinegar and reduce until it starts to caramelise. Add the wines and reduce to a jammy consistency. Season.
6. Panfry the ballotine in some clarifed butter until crispy on the outside.

TO SERVE

1. Place the red cabbage in the centre of the plate or serve separately.
2. Slice the ballotines and divide into 8 portions. Place on top of the cabbage.
3. Drizzle with sauce.

MY TIP

Ask your butcher to bone out the grouse from the back so that the breasts and legs are still attached to the skin and in one piece.

Goats Cheese Soufflé, Salad Bouquet and an Orange Dressing

INGREDIENTS (SERVES 4)

175g	goats cheese, mashed		Seasoning
150ml	milk	50ml	orange dressing
20g	butter	10ml	pistachio oil
2	shallots, minced		(see p. 52)
30ml	flour	30g	salad leaves
2	eggs	5g	almonds

METHOD

1. Sweat the minced shallot in the butter until softened. Add the flour and make a roux (see p.165).
2. Remove from heat, and add the milk slowly. Return to the heat to cook the flour slowly. When the mixture starts to become very thick, remove from the heat and pass. This sauce is known as a béchamel.
3. Add the yolk of one egg and mashed cheese to the béchamel and season.
4. Whisk the egg whites until standing, then fold into the mix.
5. Place into moulds, dusted with flaked almonds and flour, and bake in a preheated oven at 180°C for 8 minutes. Serve immediately.

Orange dressing

MY TIP

Make the orange dressing in advance. It will keep for days in the fridge.

INGREDIENTS

1	egg (yolk only)	30ml	orange juice
5g	wholegrain mustard	50ml	white wine vinegar
		100ml	olive oil

METHOD

1. Add the mustard, yolk, juice, and vinegar to a blender and blend until creamy.
2. Add the olive oil very slowly and incorporate very well. Season and chill.

TO SERVE

1. Place a soufflé on each plate.
2. Dress the lettuce leaves with the pistachio oil (optional) and place leaves with the souffle.
3. Use the orange dressing to garnish the plate.

Hot Chocolate Pudding with Chocolate Chip Ice Cream and Orange and Berry

INGREDIENTS (SERVES 8)

300g	dark chocolate		8	scoops of choc-chip ice cream (*see p. 152*)
150g	sugar			
4	eggs		2	oranges, peeled and segmented
150g	butter, melted		8	strawberries
10g	baking powder		8	blackberries
75g	flour		8	raspberries

METHOD
1. Melt the chocolate and the butter over a bain Marie.
2. Cream the sugar and the eggs together.
3. Fold this mixture into the chocolate and add the flour and the baking powder.
4. Put into individual moulds and bake in the oven at 180°C for 8 minutes.

TO SERVE
1. Garnish with ice cream, berries and orange.

Japanese Raw Beef with Escabeshe Salsa (page 33)

Japanese Raw Beef with Escabeshe Salsa (page 32)

INGREDIENTS (SERVES 8)

600g	beef fillet
50ml	mirin
50ml	soya
3 tsp	sweet chilli
1	clove of garlic
30g	honey
50ml	plum sauce
1	tomato, peeled and seeded
100g	cucumber, peeled and seeded
1	red pepper, roasted seeded and peeled
1	yellow pepper, roasted seeded and peeled
1	mango, diced
10g	shallots, minced
10ml	sherry vinegar
10ml	olive oil
1 tsp	coriander, chopped

METHOD

1. Trim all fat and sinew from the beef.
2. Make the marinade from the soya, honey, mirin, sweet chilli, crushed garlic and the plum sauce. Place the beef in the marinade and leave for 24 hours.
3. Brunoise the peppers, tomato and cucumber and add the rest of the ingredients to make the salsa.

TO SERVE

1. Slice the beef very thinly and place it in the centre of the plate.
2. Put the salsa on top and drizzle with the marinade.
3. Garnish with some balsamic reduction drops if you like. Lettuce leaves can also be used if required.

Japanese Raw Beef with
Escabeshe Salsa

Crab Soup Garnished with
Crab Claws

Baked Woodcock with
Foie Gras, Thyme Jus
and Salad

Caesar Salad

Sautéed Brill on Leeks with
an Oyster Sauce

Quail Stuffed with Crab and
Chicken, Apple Clafoutis
and a Cider Foam

Camembert Cheese,
Served with
Quince Chutney
and Banana Bread

Apple Tart Tatin

Crab Soup Garnished with Crab Claws

INGREDIENTS (SERVES 8 SMALL PORTIONS)

6	crabs	100ml	white wine
100g	mireapoix of vegetables	50ml	Pernod
1	clove of garlic	200ml	cream
2	sprigs of thyme	50g	butter
50g	fennel, roughly chopped	2	crab claws to garnish each
500ml	fish stock (*see p. 159*)		serving

METHOD

1. Boil the crabs for 12 minutes, then remove the meat and reserve the claws. About six crabs should give 350g-400g meat and 12 claws.
2. Sweat the small cut mireapoix of vegetables and the roughly chopped fennel with the garlic and thyme till soft, then add the wine and Pernod. Roast the crab shells and add with the vegetables and wine.
3. Reduce to almost nothing, add the stock and reduce this by half. Strain.
4. Add the crabmeat and cream, reduce to a soup consistency and season.
5. Blend in a robot coupe till smooth. Pass.
6. Remove the claws from the shells and sauté in some butter.
7. Serve in a soup cup and garnish with crab claws.

Baked Woodcock with Foie Gras and Truffle Salad, drizzled with a Thyme Jus

INGREDIENTS (SERVES 4)

4	woodcock
100g	puff pastry *(see p. 149)*
120g	foie gras
50g	mixed lettuce leaves
8	cherry tomatoes
50g	cucumber, diced
1tsp	white truffle oil
100ml	thyme jus *(see p.155)*
	eggwash – 1egg yoke
	50ml milk
30g	chicken mince
5g	truffle pieces

METHOD

1. Remove the legs from the woodcock. Bone the legs completely out, leaving the crowns in one piece.
2. Add 20g of the foie gras and the truffle pieces to the chicken mince, then season.
3. Stuff the woodcock legs with the mince and roll tightly into a cylinder shape. Crépinette the legs tightly.
4. Seal the legs and the crowns in some clarifed butter and roast in a hot oven at 200°C for 8 minutes.
5. Roll out the puff pastry to about 5mm thick. Cut into circles of 2.5cm diameter, and brush with eggwash. Cook with the woodcocks for 8minutes till golden brown and risen.

TO SERVE

1. Remove the breasts from the crowns and cut the legs in half.
2. Cut the tomatoes in quarters, mix with the lettuce leaves and cucumber, and dress with the oil.
3. Slice the foie gras into four pieces and seal them in a smoking hot pan for 10 seconds on each side.

4. Place the breasts and legs on the plate and put the salad and foie gras on the breast. Drizzle with the sauce.
5. Warm the sauce and garnish the plate with the pastry.

. . . .

Caesar Salad

INGREDIENTS (SERVES 4)

METHOD

60 ml	caesar dressing (*see p.47*)	20g	croutons
100g	baby cos lettuce	20g	Parmesan cheese, grated
20g	bacon		

1. Separate the leaves of the baby cos, wash and dry well.
2. Panfry the bacon and croutons until crisp.
3. Combine everything together to form a salad.

Sautéed Brill on Leeks with an Oyster Sauce (*page 38*)

Sautéed Brill on Leeks with an Oyster Sauce (see page 37)

(see page 37)

INGREDIENTS (SERVES 8)

4	fillets of brill, each about 180 gm	50ml	white wine
200g	leeks	150ml	oyster sauce (see p. 155)
50g	butter	10g	clarifed butter
		8	whole oysters, shelled

METHOD
1. Cut the leeks in half lengthwise, slice very thinly, then wash and dry them.
2. Sweat the leeks in the butter, add the wine and reduce until the wine is gone.
3. Season and keep warm.
4. Sauté the brill in the clarifed butter for about 2 minutes on each side till both sides have caramelised.

TO SERVE
1. Place the brill on top of the leeks, with the raw (or cooked, if you prefer) oyster on top.
2. Warm the oyster sauce and drizzle around.

• •

Stuffed Boneless Quail with Crab and Chicken, Apple Clafoutis and Cider Foam

INGREDIENTS (SERVES 8)

4	boneless quails	120 ml	cider foam
60g	chicken, minced	1	sheet of crépinette
60g	crabmeat (cooked)	50g	butter
90g	apple compote (see p. 59)		Oil for frying
4	apple crisps (see p. 102)		Seasoning
120ml	Clafoutis mix	5g	black truffle

METHOD

1. Mix the chicken mince with the crabmeat and 1/3 of the apple compote. Season the mix with salt and pepper.

2. Lay out the quails on the table, skin side down. Divide the chicken mix into 4, roll them into small cylinders and put them in the middle of the quails. Fold the quail meat together over it, making a tight parcel. Separate the crépinette and lay a thin layer flat on the work surface. Roll each quail in at least 2 layers of the crépinette to ensure that the quails hold their shape.

3. Butter and flour the insides of 8 small moulds. Divide half of the clafoutis mix between the moulds. Using 1/3 of the apple compote, put a small amount of it in each mould. Fill up with the rest of the clafoutis mix and cook the in the oven for 10 minutes.

4. Heat a frying pan and seal the quails in the oil and butter. Cook them in the oven at 180°c for 8 minutes and then let them rest for 4 minutes on a tray with a towel.

5. Heat the cider foam slowly, without bringing it to the boil. If it gets too hot it won't foam.

TO SERVE

1. Put the clafoutis on the 8 plates. Heat the rest of the apple compote and divide it between the plates.

2. Trim off the ends of each quail and cut in half, placing them in the centre of each plate.

3. Foam the sauce with a hand mixer, adding a small amount of milk to help it foam.

4. Carefully take the foam with a spoon and divide it between the plates.

5. Garnish each plate with an apple crisp and thin slices of truffle (optional).

4. Place on top of the moulds and eggwash.
5. Bake in an oven at 200°C for 8-10 minutes until the pastry has risen and is golden brown.
6. Turn the tarts out while hot so the pastry is now on the bottom.

TO SERVE
1. Garnish each plate with the strawberries, blackberries, fig anglaise sauce and a scoop of ice cream.
2. An apple wonton is optional as a garnish. Make the wonton the same way as a plum spring roll on page 66. Use the apple compote on page 59.

Assiette of Salmon

INGREDIENTS (SERVES 4)

60g	smoked salmon		60 ml	Herb Aioli (see p. 148)
120g	fresh salmon		5ml	Balsamic reduction
60ml	Crème de Cassis dressing (see p.147)		120g	Gravad lax of salmon (see below)
140g	crabmeat (cooked)		4	chicory leaves
1/2lt	pickling liquid (see p.115)			Scallop powder (see p.149)
60g	salmon roe		60ml	Hofmaster sauce (see p.51)
30g	mixed leaves			

Assiette of Salmon

∞∞

Sweet Potato Soup
and Crisp Prawn

∞∞

Tuna Cappaccio with Basil
and Beetroot Oil,
and a Blue Cheese Caesar
Salad

∞∞

Blini Pancakes with a
Roasted Aubergine
and Pepper Chutney

∞∞

Duo of Monkfish and Lobster

∞∞

Sautéed Scallops
with Hofmaster Sauce,
Truffle Shavings
and Frissée Salad

∞∞

Pont L'Eveque Cheese
with Grape Relish

∞∞

Chocolate and Hazelnut Cake
with Butterscotch Sauce
and a Natural Yoghurt and
Crème Fraiche Nut Terrine

METHOD

1. Trim and skin the fresh salmon and cut it into 4 squares. Bring the pickling liquid to the boil and pour it over the salmon. Let the salmon cool down in the liquid.
2. Brush the insides of 4 cappuccino cups with a little bit of water, then line with cling film, leaving some extra around the edges.
3. Carve the smoked salmon into thin slices and use to cover the inside of the cups. Make sure the salmon slices are overlapping each other, and leave enough salmon around the edge to fold over as a lid.
4. Mix the crabmeat with 2/3 of the crème de cassis dressing and season with salt and pepper. Divide the mix between the 4 cups and fold the smoked salmon over as a lid.
5. Use the cling film to tighten into small parcels then take out of the cups and remove the cling film.
6. Carve the gravad lax into long slices and divide into 4. Lay the slices flat on the work top overlapping each other and roll them into nice rosettes.

TO SERVE

1. Use the scallop powder to divide each plate into 3 sections.
2. Place the rosettes of gravad lax in one section, with a small 'teardrop' of the Hofmaster sauce beside it.
3. Place the pickled salmon in another corner and garnish with the herb aioli. Use half of the salmon roe to decorate the pickled salmon on each plate and the other half to stand up the chicory leaves on each plate as a garnish.
4. Place the smoked salmon and crab parcel in the last corner and garnish the parcel with small dressed mixed leaves.
5. Finally, garnish each plate with a line of small drops of the balsamic reduction.

. . . .

Gravad lax salmon

INGREDIENTS

20g sugar	20g rock sea salt
20ml sweet white wine	120gm salmon

METHOD

1. Make a paste from the sugar, rock sea salt and sweet white wine.
2. Place it on the salmon. Cover and marinade for 6 hours on one side before turning it over to marinade for 6 hours on the other side.
3. Remove and wash off the marinade. Use within 2 days.

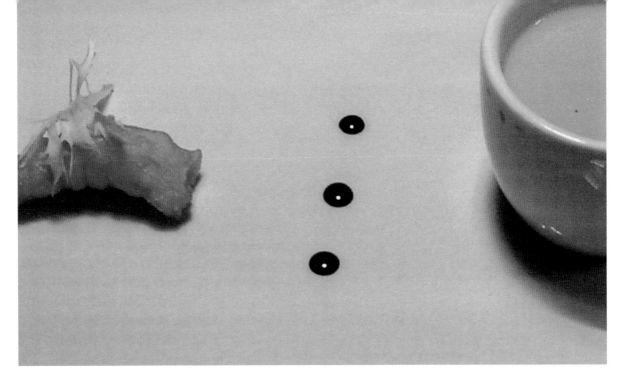

Sweet Potato Soup and Crisp Prawn

INGREDIENTS (SERVES 8)

500g	sweet potatoes		100ml	white wine
100g	onions		100ml	chicken stock (*see p.159*)
100g	leeks		500ml	cream
60g	butter		8	prawns

METHOD

1. Slice the leeks and wash them. Peel the sweet potatoes and the onions. Roughly chop them and then sweat with the leeks in the butter till soft and they start to lightly caramelise.
2. Add the wine and reduce to almost nothing.
3. Add the stock and the cream and cook until the sweet potatoes are soft.
4. Blend until smooth, pass and season to taste.

TO SERVE

1. Shallow fry the prawns crisp and serve on the side of the soup. The prawns can also be wrapped in some spring roll pastry and then fried.

Tuna Cappaccio with Basil and
Beetroot Oil and a Blue Cheese
Caesar Salad (page 47)

Tuna Cappaccio with Basil and Beetroot Oil and a Blue Cheese Caesar Salad (page 46)

INGREDIENTS (SERVES 4)

240g	round tuna steak	40ml	beetroot oil (*see p.161*)
5g	salt	80g	blue cheese
3g	pepper	20	baby cos lettuce leaves
1tsp	chopped mixed herbs	40g	croutons
30ml	olive oil	10g	butter
20ml	white wine	20g	bacon lardons
60ml	basil oil (*see p.148*)	80ml	Caesar dressing
		20g	Parmesan cheese, grated

METHOD

1. Coat the tuna with the salt, pepper, herbs, wine and olive oil and refridgerate over night.
2. Cook the bacon lardons until crisp and toss the croutons in the butter till golden brown.
3. Wash and dry the cos lettuce. Crumble the blue cheese and combine with the cos lettuce leaves, croutons and bacon lardons. Add the Caesar dressing and mix well. Sprinkle with the Parmesan cheese.
4. Remove the tuna from the fridge and slice as thinly as possible.

TO SERVE

1. Place the sliced tuna directly on to the centre of the plate - five pieces per portion should be sufficient.
2. Oil the plates with the two oils and dress the salad on top.

Caesar Dressing

INGREDIENTS

100g	mayonnaise (*see p.153*)	20g	anchovy fillets, minced or puréed
20g	Parmesan cheese, grated	1tsp	chopped parsley

METHOD

Blend all the ingredients together. Do not season as the anchovies will be naturally salty.

Blini Pancakes with a Roasted Aubergine and Pepper Chutney

INGREDIENTS (SERVES 4)

12	blini pancakes (*see p.155*)	60ml	olive oil
1	aubergine	4	garlic cloves
1	red pepper	4	shallots
1	yellow pepper		

METHOD

1. Roughly chop the aubergine and peppers. Heat the oil in a heavy pan and sauté all the ingredients. Cook uncovered in the oven at 200°C for 20 minutes.
2. Blend the cooked ingredients until smooth, then pass the purée through a tamis and season.
3. Allow the chutney to cool.

TO SERVE

Serve with hot or cold blini pancakes.

Monkfish on Paysanne of Vegetables with Lobster Sauce and Lobster on Leeks with Fig Jus (page 49)

Monkfish on Paysanne of Vegetables with Lobster Sauce and Lobster on Leeks with Fig Jus (page 48)

INGREDIENTS (SERVES 4)

4	monkfish medallions, each 50g in weight	80g	leeks, sliced, cooked and refreshed
2	cooked lobster tails	50ml	fig jus
4	cooked lobster claws	50ml	lobster sauce (see p.149)
80g	Paysanne of vegetables (see p.166)	4	Dauphine nets (see p151)
		50g	butter

METHOD

1. Cut the lobster tails in half lengthways and place in a pot with some butter over a gentle heat to warm slowly.
2. Warm the leeks and paysanne of vegetables separately in some butter and season.
3. Warm the lobster sauce and fig jus.
4. Panfry the monkfish medallions in some butter for two minutes on each side.

TO SERVE

1. Place the monkfish on the paysanne of vegetables and sauce with the lobster sauce.
2. Place one half of a lobster tail on the leeks and one claw with the fig jus.
3. Garnish the monkfish with the dauphine nets.

Fig jus

INGREDIENTS

3	fresh figs	4	black peppercorns
100ml	veal jus (see p.158)	50g	butter
3	shallots		

METHOD

1. Sweat the shallots and peppercorns in the butter till soft.
2. Add the chopped figs and cook for two minutes until the figs break down to a pulp.
3. Add the veal jus and reduce to a coating consistency. Pass and season.

Sautéed Scallops with Frisée Salad, Hofmaster Sauce and Truffle Shavings

INGREDIENTS (SERVES 8)

16	scallops	60g	frisée lettuce
100g	cucumber	5g	truffle shavings
2	tomatoes	100g	Hofmaster sauce
		20ml	Balsamic dressing (*see p.147*)

METHOD

1. Peel, deseed and brunoise the cucumber and the tomatoes.
2. Clean and pick the lettuce and add the cucumber and tomatoes. Dress with some balsamic dressing.
3. Sauté the scallops in some clarified butter for 30 seconds each side until caramelised.

→

TO SERVE

1. Drizzle the Hofmaster sauce around the scallops.
2. Garnish with the truffle shavings and dressed leaves.

Hofmaster Sauce

INGREDIENTS

200ml olive oil	70g sweet mustard
1 egg yolk	20g sugar
100ml sherry vinegar	2 tsp chopped dill

METHOD

1. Blend the egg yolk, vinegar and mustard in the blender. Add the sugar and then add the olive oil slowly to form a mayonnaise.
2. Finish the sauce with the dill and seasoning.

. . . .

Pont L'eveque Cheese with a Grape Relish, Lamb's Lettuce and Pistachio Oil

INGREDIENTS (SERVES 4)
50g grape relish (*see p61*)
160g Pont l'eveque cheese
8 sprigs of lamb's lettuce
10ml pistachio oil

TO SERVE

1. Cut the cheese into slices and serve with two sprigs of lamb's lettuce per portion.
2. Dress the plates with the grape relish and pistachio oil.

Pistachio Oil

INGREDIENTS

100g   pistachio nuts
100ml olive oil

METHOD

1.   Place the nuts and oil in a pot and slowly bring to a temperature of 60-70°C for 20 minutes.
2.   Pour into a blender and mix to a pulp.

....

Chocolate and Hazelnut Cake with a Butterscotch Sauce and a Natural Yoghurt and Crème Fraiche Nut Terrine

INGREDIENTS (SERVES 4)

115g	soft butter	4	yoghurt and crème fraiche terrines
100g	icing sugar		
2	eggs	100ml	butterscotch sauce (see p.54)
70g	dark chocolate	8	blackberries
60g	flour	4	strawberries
100g	hazelnuts	150g	ganache (see p.53)

METHOD

1.   To make the chocolate cake, first melt the chocolate over a bain Marie.
2.   Sabayon the butter, sugar and the eggs together till light and fluffy.
3.   Crush the hazelnuts and add to the chocolate.
4.   Add the Sabayon to the chocolate, incorporate well and fold in the flour.
5.   Pour into a terrine that has been lined with paper and bake in a preheated oven at 180°C for 20-30 minutes.
6.   Check that the cake is cooked by gently piercing its centre with a knife - if the blade comes out clean, the cake is ready.
3.   Remove the cake from the terrine and allow to cool.
4.   Slice the cake into 1 cm thick slices.
5.   Pour the ganache mix over the slices, smoothing the top with a palate knife. Allow to set in the fridge.

Ganache

INGREDIENTS
100g   dark chocolate
40g   butter
40ml cream

METHOD
1.   Place the ingredients in a bain Marie and melt till fully incorporated. The resulting mix will be shiny and ideal for coating cakes and desserts.

Natural Yoghurt and Crème Fraiche Nut Terrine

INGREDIENTS (SERVES 4)

50g	crème fraiche	1	leaf of gelatine
50g	natural yoghurt	50g	panache of nuts
50g	cream		

METHOD
1. Place the gelatine in cold water to soften.
2. Add the soft gelatine to a little of the cream and place on the heat to dissolve.
3. Mix all the ingredients together and add the gelatine, incorporating it well.
4. Pour into the moulds (6-8) and allow to set in the fridge.

Butterscotch Sauce

INGREDIENTS

40ml	water	230ml	cream
50g	sugar	75g	butter

METHOD
1. Make a caramel from the sugar and the water. The more you colour the caramel the darker your finished sauce will become.
2. Remove caramel from the heat and add the cream slowly. The mix will bubble and resemble toffee so put it back on the heat to melt and incorporate the ingredients. Add the butter last.

N.B. *Be very careful with the caramel as it will give you a nasty burn.*

TO SERVE
1. When the ganache has set, cut the slices of cake into circles of 2cm in diameter.
2. Garnish with the terrine, berries and butterscotch sauce.

←
Petit Fours
(see pages 156-157)

Chocolate Macaroons

INGREDIENTS

120g   egg white
50g   caster sugar
250g   icing sugar
125g   ground almonds
25g   Cacao

1. Whisk egg whites until soft peaks, add the sugar and whisk until stiff peaks.
2. Mix the rest of the ingredients and sieve.
3. Fold the dry ingredients in to the meringue.
4. Pipe small discs on to greaseproof paper and bake in oven at 150°C for 12-16 minutes.

MY TIP
These cakes are equally tasty made with milk or white chocolate, or a selection of cakes may be used as in photo on page 53.

Loin of Lamb Marinaded in Ginger with a Ginger Jus and Yorkshire Pudding (*page 63*)

Loin of Rabbit with Chorizo Mousse, Rillette, Spring Roll, Fig Compote and a Rosemary Jus

INGREDIENTS (SERVES 4)

1	whole rabbit		crépinette (*see Glossary p.164*)
1	chorizo sausage	100ml	rosemary jus
2	spring roll wrappers	4tsp	fig compote
1lt	confit oil		Seasoning

METHOD

1. Remove the 4 legs from the whole rabbit, leaving the centre piece. The centre piece is know as the loins. Remove the loins from the bone and remove the sinew.
2. Place the legs of the rabbit in the confit oil and cook at 80°C for two hours.
3. When the confit has cooled, remove all the meat and reserve, dividing it in two portions.
4. Allow the confit oil to settle before spooning out the jelly that has settled on the bottom. Using one portion of the reserved meat, combine 10g of this jelly and 10g

→

Loin of Rabbit with Chorizo
Mousse, Rillette,
Spring Roll, Fig Compote and a
Rosemary Jus

Poached Foie Gras in Cider,
Cider Jelly,
Apple Compote and
a Shot of Apple Snaps

Game Terrine with Grape
Relish, Coriander
Oil and Cumberland Sauce

Peach Sorbet

Loin of Kangaroo with
Red Currant Jus
and a Red Onion Tart

Loin of Lamb Marinaded in
Ginger, with a Ginger Jus
and Yorkshire Pudding

Irish Cheddar, Pickled
Cucumber and Carrot,
and Parsley Oil

Orange and Cointreau Parfait,
with PlumSpring Rolls
and Baileys Anglaise Sauce

of the confit oil with every 100g of meat. Roll this in to a cylinder shape using cling film. Refrigerate to set. This is the rillette.

5. Cut the two spring roll wrappers in half and make four spring rolls with the other portion of the reserved meat.
6. Remove the skin from the chorizo sausage and purée the meat to a smooth mousse in a blender. Place the mousse on the rabbit loins and wrap them in the crépinette.
7. Panfry the stuffed rabbit loins, then cook in the oven at 180°C for four minutes.
8. Warm the sauce and deep-fry the spring rolls.

TO SERVE
1. Slice the rillette and lightly warm. Cut the loins into 8 pieces.
2. Deep fry the spring rolls.
3. Make a small mixed salad as garnish, then dress the plates with rosemary jus and fig compote.

Fig compote

INGREDIENTS

200g figs, fresh or dried	100ml red wine	50g sugar

METHOD
1. Combine the wine and sugar in a saucepan and reduce by half.
2. Add the figs and reduce to a compote, a similar consistency to jam.

Rosemary jus

INGREDIENTS

100ml veal jus (see p.158)		6	black peppercorns
3	sprigs of rosemary	50g	butter
3	shallots	5ml	red wine

METHOD
1. Sweat the shallots in the butter with the peppercorns until soft. Add rosemary.
2. Add the red wine and reduce by two thirds and then add the jus and reduce further by half.
3. Season and pass.

5

Poached Foie Gras in Cider, Cider Jelly, Apple Compote and a Shot of Apple Snaps

INGREDIENTS (SERVES 4)

400g	foie gras
300ml	cider
2	apples
10g	honey
50g	sugar
50ml	white wine
1	leaf of gelatine
	Seasoning

METHOD

1. Clean all sinew and arteries from the foie gras and marinade it in half the cider, with seasoning, for 24 hours.
2. Soak the gelatine leaf in cold water. Bring 150ml of cider to the boil, add the soaked gelatine leaf and place in the fridge until it sets. Once set, brake it up with a fork.
3. Remove the foie gras from the fridge after 24 hours, discard marinade and roll tightly in cling film into a cylinder of one inch in diameter. Poach in boiling water for three minutes, then put in iced water to cool quickly.
4. To make the compote, peel and core the apples and dice them into very small cubes.
5. Lightly caramelise the sugar, honey and white wine and add the apples. Cook and reduce to a jam consistency but with a bite in the apples. If the apples are cooking more quickly than the liquid is reducing, remove the apples and replace them when the liquid is the right consistency.

TO SERVE

1. Slice the foie gras and quenelle compote when cold.
2. Garnish the plate with some cider jelly and serve with a glass of apple snaps.

Game Terrine with Grape Relish and Coriander Oil

INGREDIENTS
(SERVES 10 /MAKES 2KG TERRINE)

100g	Parma ham		100g	venison loin
1kg	chicken mince		10ml	coriander oil
100g	black pudding		100g	grape relish
1	duck breast		50ml	Cumberland sauce
8	snipe breasts			

METHOD

1. Line a 2kg terrine with cling film, then line it again with sliced Parma ham.
2. Mince the black pudding, add it to the chicken mince and season.
3. Smoke the duck breast for five minutes so that it is still medium rare *see p 167*. Slice it thinly lengthways.
4. Panfry the venison loin and snipe breasts so that they are sealed on the outside and rare on the inside.
5. Place some of the duck on top of the Parma ham in the terrine, and then some mince. Start layering the terrine with the duck and the mince, with the snipe and the venison in the centre. Cover with the mince on top and cover with Parma ham. Place foil on top and bake in a bain Marie in the oven at 160°C for 40 minutes.

TO SERVE

1. Allow the terrine to cool, then cut it into slices about one cm thick.
2. Garnish the plate with the grape relish, Cumberland sauce and some coriander oil.

Grape Relish

INGREDIENTS

300g	red seedless grapes	30g	honey
50g	sugar	50ml	red wine

METHOD

1. Add the sugar, wine and the honey to a pot and reduce to a glaze. Add 5g of All Spice (optional).
2. Slice the grapes in half and add to the glaze. Cook for 5 minutes so that the relish is the consistency of jam.
3. Remove from heat and allow to cool.

Cumberland Sauce

INGREDIENTS

200ml	red currant jelly	1tsp	ginger
1	orange, zest and juice	70ml	port wine
1	lemon, zest and juice		

METHOD

1. Add all the ingredients to a heavy pot and allow to reduce at a simmer until the volume reduces by about one third. The consistency should be like honey.
2. Cool and keep in a clean jar for up to a month.

Peach Sorbet

INGREDIENTS (SERVES 8)

175g	sugar	2g	sorbet stabilizer
250ml	water	325g	peach purée

METHOD

Boil the water, sugar and stabilizer for 3 minutes and add the purée and allow to cool. Finish in an ice cream machine and freeze.

METHOD

1. Boil the whole oranges unpeeled for one hour till completely soft in the sugar syrup. Remove from the syrup and blend till smooth. Pass through tamis.
2. Sabayon the eggs and sugar together and add the Cointreau.
3. Whisk the cream to semi peak and fold everything together into a creamy consistency.
4. Pour into a terrine lined with cling film and freeze.
5. Make the sauce by mixing together the Bailey's liqueur and vanilla anglaise.

TO SERVE

1. Deep fry the plum spring rolls till golden brown.
2. Serve with a slice of parfait and some berries. Drizzle with sauce.

Plum Spring Rolls

INGREDIENTS

6	plums
50g	sugar
50ml	white wine
20g	honey
8	spring roll wrappers

METHOD

1. Remove the stones from the plums and chop the plums very finely.
2. Lightly caramelise the sugar, honey and wine, add the plums and cook to a jammy consistency by reducing until the liquid is almost gone.
3. When completely cooled, wrap tightly in the spring roll wrappers and deep fry till golden brown.

Orange and Cointreau Parfait with Plum Spring Rolls and Baileys Anglaise Sauce (page 65)

Pork Fillet, Suckling Pig Rillette, Parma Ham Crisp and Apple Compote with a Cumin Jus (page 73)

Smoked Haddock and Spinach Mille Feuille, with a Pernod Sauce

INGREDIENTS (SERVES 4)

320g	smoked haddock	8	Dauphine nets	*(see p. 151)*
60g	spinach	100ml	Pernod sauce	*(see p. 111)*
50g	butter	10g	garlic and basil cress	

METHOD

1. Remove the pin bones from the fish and cook in some simmering water for approximately 6 minutes until the fish is cooked.
2. Remove from the water, flake the flesh from the skin and sauté it with the spinach in the butter. Season.

TO SERVE

1. Warm the Pernod sauce and place the haddock and spinach in the centre of the plate.
2. Place the Dauphine nets on top and then some cress on top of the nets.
3. Drizzle with the sauce.

Minted Pea Soup with a Mushroom Wonton

INGREDIENTS (SERVES 8)

500g	peas
50g	onions
50g	leeks
50g	celeriac
100g	butter
100ml	white wine
200ml	chicken or vegetable stock (*see pgs 158/159*)
300ml	cream
30g	mint leaves
80g	mushroom duxelle (*see p. 150*)
1 pkt	wonton wrappers (about 16 sheets)
	Egg wash

MY TIP

Wonton wrappers are about two inches square and are available in packs of 20-25 in good delicatessens, leading supermarkets or Asian shops.

METHOD

1. Cut the vegetables into small mireapoix, rinse under cold running water to clean. Dry and sweat in the butter till soft.
2. Add the fresh peas and cook for five minutes, then add the wine and reduce by half.
3. Pour in the chicken or vegetable stock and cook for a further 40 minutes.
4. Add the cream and reduce to a coating consistency.
5. Purée to a smooth liquid and pass. Season.
6. To make each wonton, egg wash a wonton wrapper and place another on top.
7. Put 10g of mushroom duxelle on top and fold into a triangle, sealing the sides as you go.
8. Deep fry gently until golden brown.

TO SERVE

1. Add the mint to the soup at the last minute, blend and serve with the mushroom wonton.

Crisp Polenta and Goat's Cheese Stack, with a Parmesan Crisp and Pickled Vegetables

INGREDIENTS (SERVES 8)

500g	Polenta
50ml	white wine vinegar
450ml	water
100ml	Mirin
30g	frisée lettuce
120g	goat's cheese
40g	carrots parisienne
40g	courgettes parisienne
40g	turnip parisienne
40g	cucumber parisienne
40g	swede parisienne
15g	butter
100g	caster sugar
100ml	white wine vinegar
100g	Parmesan cheese, grated
10ml	Balsamic dressing (see p.147)
10ml	herb oil

METHOD

1. Bring the water, mirin and 50ml of white wine vinegar to the boil, add the polenta and cook on a slow heat for 10 minutes. Season. Place in a 1 cm deep tray, level out and refrigerate.

2. When cold, cut into rounds of the same diameter as the goat's cheese.16 in total

3. Cook the vegetables separately in boiling salted water – the carrots for 3 minutes, the courgettes for 1 minute, the turnips and swede for 3 minutes. Strain and refresh each of them.

4. Bring 100ml vinegar and sugar to the boil, remove from the heat and add all the parisienne vegetables, including the cucumber, to the liquid. Allow to cool. These are your pickled vegetables.

$\longrightarrow$

5. Warm 8 slices of goat's cheese in the oven at 180°C for 2 minutes.
6. Deep-fry 8 slices of the polenta until crispy and golden brown.

TO SERVE

1. To make the Parmesan crisps, sprinkle the grated cheese in 2.5cm rounds on sill mats and cook in the oven at 180°C till golden brown, about two minutes. Allow to cool and become crisp.
2. Place a slice of goat's cheese between two slices of polenta and arrange the vegetables around them.
3. Garnish the plates with a little herb oil, Balsamic dressing and a Parmesan crisp.

Mixed Salad Leaves

Use a variety of lettuce and add dressing to your taste

Smoked Crisp Sea Bass on Lobster Ravioli, Chablis Sauce and Vanilla Jus

INGREDIENTS (SERVES 4)

4   fillets of sea bass, each about 90g
4   lobster ravioli (*see p. 150*)
70ml   chablis sauce (*see p. 155*)
50ml   vanilla jus (*see p. 152*)
50g   butter
1 tsp   scallop roe powder (*see p. 149*)

METHOD
1. Place the fillets in the smoker and smoke for three minutes, then remove. (*See page 167*)
2. Panfry the fillets in some clarifed butter till the skins are crispy – 2 mins on skin side 30 secs on other side.
3. Cook the raviolis for four minutes in boiling salted water.

TO SERVE
1. Warm the sauces and foam the chablis sauce.
2. Place the fillet on the ravioli and sauce with the chablis.
3. Drizzle with the vanilla jus and garnish with the scallop roe powder.

. . . .

Pork Fillet, Suckling Pig Rillette, Parma Ham Crisp and Apple Compote with a Cumin Jus (page 68)

INGREDIENTS (SERVES 8)

240g   pork fillet
240g   pig rillette
8   slices of Parma ham

100g   apple compote (*see p. 59*)
80g   sliced leeks
100ml cumin jus

→

1. The rillette is made in the usual way. Confit the whole suckling pig for 5 to 6 hours. Remove all the meat, discard all the fat and bones, and reserve the meat. Process the meat into a cylinder and set in the fridge. *(See duck confit page 15)*
2. Slice the leeks thinly, rinse well and then sauté for about 3 minutes.
3. Panfry the pork fillet to seal the meat and roast for 6 to 8 minutes. Fry the Parma ham until it is crispy.

TO SERVE
1. Warm the apple chutney and the cumin jus.
2. Slice the rillette and reheat the leeks in some butter.
3. Cut the pork fillet into 8 slices and place on the leeks.
4. Place the chutney beside the pork and the Parma ham beside that.
5. Add a slice of the rillette to the plate and drizzle with the sauce.

Cumin jus

INGREDIENTS

100g	veal jus *(see p.158)*	3	shallots
50g	butter	5	black peppercorns
		5g	cumin seeds

METHOD
1. Sweat the shallots and peppercorns in the butter till soft. Add the cumin seeds and the jus.
2. Reduce to a coating consistency and season. Pass.

. . . .

Chèvre Cheese with Pickled Beetroots

INGREDIENTS (SERVES 8)

200g	chèvre cheese	10ml	parsley oil *(see p.148)*
16	pickled baby beetroots *(see p. 81)*	30g	mixed lettuce

TO SERVE
1. Cut the cheese into wedges and serve with two pickled beetroots for each portion.
2. Dress the plates with some parsley oil and dressed lettuce.

Tartlet of Grapes and Chiboust of Pear Cream
with Pink Grapefruit Granite (see following page)

Tartlet of Grapes and Chiboust of Pear Cream with Pink Grapefruit Granite (page 75)

(page 75)

INGREDIENTS (SERVES 4)

Pastry for Tartlet:

125g	butter
25g	flour
1	egg
100g	caster sugar

Tartlet Mix:

3	eggs
70g	caster sugar
1	vanilla pod
150ml	milk
150ml	cream
100g	white or black grapes

METHOD

1. To make the pastry, mix soft butter with the flour until incorporated.
2. Whisk egg and sugar together and add to mix.
3. Knead well until a smooth dough is formed.
4. Allow to rest for 2 hours. Roll out until 3 mm thick and use to line individual cake moulds.
5. Blind bake in oven at 180°C for 6 minutes.
6. Mix all the tartlet mix ingredients together and pass through sieve.
7. Add grapes to the pastry moulds and then pour in the mix.
8. Cook in the oven at 180°C for about 8 minutes until the mix sets like a quiche.
9. Remove from oven and cool.

Chiboust of Pear

INGREDIENTS (SERVES 4)

50g	caster sugar
75g	pear purée
1	egg yolk
25g	sugar
15g	flour
1	leaf of gelatine
2	egg whites
83g	sugar

METHOD

1. Heat pear purée and cream together and bring to the boil. Add egg yolks, 50g of sugar and sieved flour to the purée and mix well. Return to the heat, whisking all the time until thickened. This is crème patissiere. Keep warm.
2. Heat 30g of sugar to 118°C.
3. Add the soaked gelatine to the sugar.
4. Whisk egg whites to stiff peaks and add the hot sugar very slowly to form an Italian meringue.
5. Add meringue to crème patissiere and fold in until smooth. Place in moulds and set in fridge.
6. When cool and set, remove from moulds and place on top of grape tart.
7. Sprinkle with rest of caster sugar and caramelise with blowtorch or grill.

Pink Grapefruit Granite

INGREDIENTS

200g   pink grapefruit, peeled and pith removed
10g   lemon juice
70g   caster sugar
70ml   champagne

METHOD

1. Combine all the ingredients and bring to the boil. Place in freezer. As it begins to set, whisk so that the ice crystal remains separated like crushed ice.

Kitchen Staff at Locks

Sautéed Scallops with Pickled Beetroot and a
Bouillabaisse Dressing (following page)

Sautéed Scallops with Pickled Beetroot and a Bouillabaisse Dressing
(page 80)

INGREDIENTS (SERVES 8)

16	king scallops, medium		80ml	bouillabaisse dressing
16	baby beetroots		10ml	herb oil (see p.148)
100ml	white wine vinegar		10ml	Balsamic reduction (see p.147)
300ml	water		30g	mixed lettuce
200g	caster sugar			

METHOD

1. Cook the beetroots in their skins in boiling water until soft and then peel while still hot.
2. Add the sugar to the vinegar and water, and bring to the boil. This is the pickling brine. Add the peeled beetroots and leave them in the liquid until it goes cold.
3. Sauté the scallops in some clarifed butter for 30 seconds on each side.

TO SERVE

1. Garnish with lettuce, bouillabaisse dressing, herb oil and the Balsamic reduction, and serve with the beetroot.

Bouillabaisse dressing

INGREDIENTS

500ml	crab shells		50ml	Pernod
200g	small mireapoix		300ml	olive oil
50g	tomato trimming		1lt	water
30g	tomato purée		50g	butter
100ml	white wine		200g	fish bones

METHOD

1. Roast the crab shells in the oven.
2. In a heavy pan, sauté the mireapoix, tomato and the purée and then add the roasted shells with the fish bones. Add the wine and the Pernod and reduce by half.

→

Sautéed Scallops with Pickled Beetroot and a Bouillabaisse Dressing

Root Vegetable Soup with a Goat's Cheese Wonton

Terrine of Pig's Cheek and Lamb's Tongue with Balsamic Vinegar and Beetroot Dressing

Chocolate Sorbet

Salmon Zubabacka Puff Pastry Roll with Risotto, Egg and Caviar, and a White Wine Sauce

Honeyed Duck Breast, Pithivier of Confit Leg, Carrot and Cumin Mousse with a Grapefruit Sauce

Brie with Croutons, Grape Relish and a Walnut Dressing

Praline Pyramid with Citrus Sauce

3. Cover this with sufficient water to cover the shells and bones and simmer for two hours. Strain the liquid.
4. Return the liquid to the stove and reduce to about 200ml. Remove from the heat, strain and cool.
5. Add the olive oil very slowly to the liquid and incorporate till smooth and creamy. Season.

....

Root Vegetable Soup with a Goat's Cheese Wonton

INGREDIENTS (SERVES 8)

500g	root vegetable mireapoix of parsnip, celeriac, carrots and turnip
100g	leeks and onions (in total)
50g	butter
100ml	white wine
500ml	cream
2 tsp	white truffle oil
	Seasoning
40g	goat's cheese
8	wonton wrappers
	Egg wash

METHOD
1. Sweat the mireapoix of root vegetables in the butter with the leeks and onions till softened.
2. Add the wine and reduce by half. Add the cream and cook to a pulp.
3. When cooked, put in a blender and purée. Pass till smooth. Season.
4. Add the truffle oil.
5. Mash the goat's cheese and divide between 8 wonton wrappers.
6. Seal tightly and egg wash. Deep fry.

TO SERVE
1. Place into soup cup and garnish with wonton.

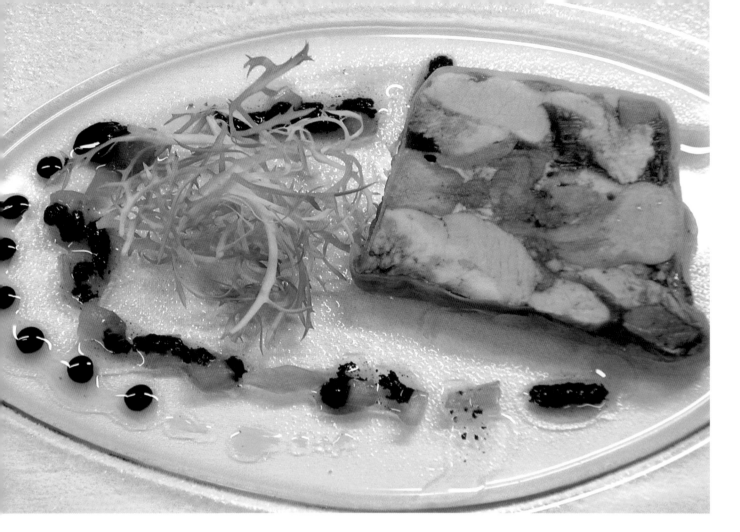

Terrine of Pig's Cheek and Lamb's Tongue with a Balsamic Reduction and Beetroot Dressing

INGREDIENTS (SERVES ABOUT 16)

1kg	lamb's tongue	100ml	veal jus (see p.158)
1kg	pig's cheeks	5ml	Balsamic reduction (see p.147)
100g	small mireapoix	10ml	basil oil (see p.148)
100ml	white wine vinegar	10ml	beetroot dressing (see p.161)
500ml	confit oil	30g	frisée lettuce
1	leek		

→

METHOD

1. Cover the lamb's tongue with water and add the mireapoix and vinegar. Simmer for 2 hours.
2. Remove the tongues and peel off the skin while still hot.
3. At the same time, confit the pig's cheek for 2 hours in the oven at 70°C. Remove all the fat but leave the cheeks whole.
4. Slice the leek lengthways and clean. Blanch and refresh.
5. Line a 2kg terrine with cling film and then two-thirds of the leeks.
6. Place the pig's cheeks and lamb's tongues with the melted veal jus into the terrine and cover with the remaining leeks.
7. Put a weighted terrine on top so that the terrine is pressed down and will compact, then place in a fridge to set for six hours.

TO SERVE

1. Slice the terrine and garnish with frisée lettuce, basil oil, balsamic reduction and the beetroot dressing.

••

Salmon 'Zubabacka' Puff Pastry Roll with Risotto, Egg and Caviar, and a White Wine Sauce

INGREDIENTS (SERVES 4)

4	fillets of salmon, each about 80g	40g	lumpfish caviar
100g	puff pastry (see p.149)	100ml	white wine sauce
100g	risotto (see p.152)		Egg wash
2	eggs	50g	butter

METHOD

1. Clean the salmon fillet by removing all the skin, black under the skin and all pin bones.
2. Seal the fillets in the butter but do not cook.
3. Hard boil the eggs for 6 minutes.
4. Roll out the puff pastry 3mm thick and cut into 4 squares of about 15-20cm.

→

5. Place the salmon on the puff pastry, followed by the risotto and sliced hard boiled egg. Top with the caviar.
6. Wrap everything into a parcel and egg wash.
7. Bake in the oven at 180°C for 15 minutes till golden brown.

TO SERVE
1. Slice the puff pastry in half and sauce.

White Wine Sauce

INGREDIENTS

100ml cream
50ml   white wine
3   shallots
6   black peppercorns
50g   butter

METHOD
1. Sweat the onions and peppercorns in butter. Add white wine and reduce by two-thirds.
2. Add the cream and reduce by one-third.
3. Pass and season.

Chocolate Sorbet

INGREDIENTS (SERVES 8)

175g caster sugar	325gm melted chocolate
250ml water	50ml Tia Maria liqueur
2g stabilizer	

METHOD
1. Put the sugar, water and the stabilizer in a saucepan and bring to the boil for 3 minutes.
2. Add the rest of the ingredients and finish in a ice cream machine. Freeze.

Honeyed Duck Breast, Pithivier of Confit Leg, Carrot and Cumin Mousse with a Grapefruit Sauce

INGREDIENTS (SERVES 4)

2	margret duck breasts	200g	carrots
2	duck legs	20ml	honey
500ml	confit oil	50g	butter
100g	puff pastry	Egg wash	
5g	cumin seeds		

METHOD

1. Confit the legs in the confit oil in the oven at 70°C for about 2 hours. Allow to cool. Remove the meat and reserve.
2. Roll out the puff pastry about 5mm thick. Cut into 4 circles of 4 cm diameter to use as the base. Roll out another 4 circles about 6 cm diameter for the tops.
3. Egg wash the bases and place the leg meat on top. Cover with the tops and seal the edges. Finish by egg washing. These are called Pithivier.
4. Boil the carrots in salted water until soft. Strain, purée until very smooth and pass through a tamis. Add the butter, season and add the cumin seeds.
5. Clean the duck breasts of all excess fat and score the fat side. Place the honey in a pan and caramelise lightly before adding the breasts. Coat and caramelise the breasts and finish in a hot oven for 8 minutes.
6. Cook the Pithivier in the oven at 200°C for six minutes till golden brown.

TO SERVE

1. Warm 100ml of grapefruit sauce and garnish plate.
2. Quennel the carrot and cumin mousse. Slice the duck breasts. Sauce.

Grapefruit sauce

INGREDIENTS

3	shallots, sliced	50ml	red wine
6	black peppercorns	50ml	grapefruit juice
50g	butter	100ml	duck jus (see p.159)

Brie with Croutons, Grape Relish
and a Walnut Dressing (page 88)

Nougat Praline Pyramid with Citrus
Sauce and Pistachio Macaroons
(page 89)

Pistachio Macaroons

INGREDIENTS

120g   egg whites
50g   caster sugar
250g   icing sugar
75g   ground almonds
50g   ground pistachio nuts

METHOD
1. Whisk egg whites and sugar together until it forms stiff peaks.
2. Pass the remaining ingredients through a tamis or a sieve.
3. Fold the dry ingredients in to the meringue.
4. Pipe into small discs on greaseproof paper and bake in the oven at 150°C for 12-16 minutes.

Praline mix

INGREDIENTS

20g   hazelnuts
20g   pinenuts
20g   pistachio
20g   walnuts
20g   almonds
50ml   water
150g   sugar

METHOD
1. Reduce the sugar and water to a caramel and add all the nuts. Allow to set.
2. When set, put into a blender and crush to a powder, like shattered glass.

Potato Gnocchi with Irish Bacon and a Chanterelle Cream (page 94)

2. Parisienne the carrot, courgette and turnip and cook each separately. Refresh.
3. Sauté the potato in some clarified butter till golden and crisp.
4. Panfry the monkfish and finish in the oven at 180°C for 5 minutes.

TO SERVE
1. Warm the vegetables and add the potatoes.
2. Slice the monkfish and warm the curry sauce.
3. Place the vegetables and potato on the sliced monkfish. Sauce.

Curry Sauce

INGREDIENTS

3	shallots, finely chopped	100ml	white wine
50g	butter	1tsp	green curry paste
6	black peppercorns	150ml	cream

METHOD
1. Sweat the shallots and peppercorns in the butter till soft. Add the wine and reduce to almost nothing.
2. Add the green curry paste and cream. Reduce to a coating consistency. Season and pass.

Roast Pheasant with a Grape Relish, Baby Vegetables and Dauphine Potatoes

INGREDIENTS (SERVES 4)

2	pheasants
4	baby carrots
4	baby leeks
4	baby turnips
100g	Dauphine potatoes mix (see p.151)
100g	butter
	Seasoning
80g	grape relish
60ml	pheasant jus (see p.159)

METHOD

1. Peel and clean the vegetables. Blanch and refresh. Cook al dente.
2. Roast the two pheasants in the oven at 200°c for 15-20 minutes. When cooked, allow them to rest for 5 minutes before removing the breasts and legs.
3. Shape Dauphine potatoes and deep fry for about 1 minute, until golden brown. The legs can also be ballotines like in the photograph on page 29.

TO SERVE

1. Warm the vegetables in 50g butter and finish. Warm the pheasant jus with 50g butter and warm the grape relish.
2. Arrange the breast and leg in the centre of the plate. Place the dauphine potatoes and the vegetables around the meat and drizzle with the sauce.
3. Place the relish on the side of the plate, or serve separately.

Grape Relish

MY TIP
Sometimes a lot of liquid comes out of the grapes. If this happens, remove the grapes and allow to reduce. Then add the grapes at the end.

INGREDIENTS

250g	green seedless grapes		3	Star Anaise
250g	black seedless grapes		20g	honey
50ml	white wine		5g	All spice
100g	caster sugar			

→

METHOD

1. Put the wine, sugar, star anaise and honey in a saucepan and caramelise slightly.
2. Slice the grapes in half and add to the saucepan. Add all spice.
3. Cook completely until there is almost no liquid left. Remove and allow to cool.
4. The relish should be of a jammy consistency.

. . . .

Lavender Crème Brûlée with Jasmine Ice Cream

INGREDIENTS (SERVES 8)

500ml	cream	4	scoops of Jasmine ice cream
250ml	milk		
10g	lavender leaves		
3ml	lavender essence	12	raspberries
110g	caster sugar	8	tuiles
6	egg yolks		*(see p.155)*

METHOD

1. Cream the sugar and the yolks together and add everything else. Leave in the fridge for 4 hours to rest.
2. Cook in individual shallow moulds in a bain Marie in the oven at 120°C for about 20-30 minutes. It is cooked when it is firm. Do not overcook or it will scramble.
3. Remove from the bain Marie when cooked and allow to cool in the fridge.

TO SERVE

1. To brûlée, sprinkle some brown sugar on top of each and place under the grill until the top is golden brown. Allow to set hard. Alternatively, use a blowtorch.
2. Serve with tuile, jasmine ice cream and raspberries.

Poached Pear Stuffed with a Panache of Nuts, Wrapped in Filo Pastry and Lightly Fried, with a Prune Ice Cream and Vanilla Anglaise (following page)

Jasmine ice cream

INGREDIENTS

500ml vanilla anglaise (*see p.102*)

| 30ml | Jasmine leaves |
| 10ml | Jasmine essence |

METHOD
1. Combine all the ingredients. Finish in an ice cream machine.

MY TIP

If you cannot get Jasmine essence or leaves, diffuse a Jasmine tea bag with the milk when making the vanilla anglaise.

Poached Pear Stuffed with a Panache of Nuts, Wrapped in Filo Pastry and Lightly Fried, with a Prune Ice Cream and Vanilla Anglaise (page 100)

INGREDIENTS (SERVES 4)

4	pears
20g	hazelnuts
20g	pistachio nuts
20g	walnuts
20g	pinenuts
70ml	water
500ml	white wine

70g	sugar
2	star anaise
2	sheets of filo pastry
4	scoops prune ice cream
100ml	vanilla anglaise
4	strawberries
8	blackberries
4	banana crisps

METHOD
1. To make the panache of nuts, boil the water and the sugar together for 4 minutes. Add the nuts to this and purée in a blender. The nuts will absorb all the liquid.
2. Peel the pears and remove the cores, keeping them whole. Poach in the white wine, sugar and star anise until soft. Allow to cool. Leave some bite in the pears.
3. Stuff the centres of the pears with the nuts and wrap each in a half a sheet of filo pastry. Tie with string to hold together.
4. Deep fry them until golden brown and dry off any excess fat.

TO SERVE
1. Remove the string from the pears. Garnish with vanilla anglaise, prune ice cream, berries and banana crisps.

Vanilla anglaise

INGREDIENTS

350ml	milk	2	vanilla pods
150ml	cream	4	egg yolks
50g	caster sugar		

METHOD

1. Whisk the sugar and egg yolks together to make a light and fluffy sabayon.
2. Bring the milk, cream and vanilla pods to the boil. Remove from the heat and add to the sabayon. Whisk together.
3. Return to the stove over a bain Marie, at a low heat. Using a wooden spoon, stir the sauce slowly and allow to thicken. The sauce is ready when it coats the back of the spoon. Do not overheat the sauce and scramble the eggs.
4. Strain and allow to cool.

Banana, apple or pineapple crisps

INGREDIENTS

1	banana, apple or pineapple	100ml sugar syrup

METHOD

1. Make a stock syrup using equal quantities of sugar and water. Boil for 4 minutes. Allow to cool.
2. Slice the fruit as thinly as possible on a mandaline and dip in the syrup. Place on sill mats. Dry in the oven at 50°C until completely dry, probably between 5 and 6 hours, depending on the fruit.

Prune Ice Cream

NGREDIENTS

500ml vanilla anglaise (see above)	100g	prunes, chopped (prune stones removed)

METHOD

1. Put the vanilla anglaise into an ice cream machine. Once it starts to thicken and become creamy, add the prunes.
2. When finished, place in the freezer.

Irish Smoked Salmon and Crab Parcel, Served with Orange and Caviar

INGREDIENTS (SERVES 4)

200g	sliced smoked salmon
200g	crab meat, cooked and shelled
40g	crème fraiche
1	oranges
4 tsp	caviar (or a cheaper option)
30g	frisée lettuce
4	Parmesan crisps (*see p.160*)

METHOD

1. Line a clean muffin tin with cling film. Then line 4 of the holes with the sliced smoked salmon.
2. Bind the crab meat with the crème fraiche and segmented chopped orange. Season.
3. Place the meat into the lined holes and cover with the salmon. Make sure that the crab is completely covered by the salmon.

TO SERVE

1. Place the crisp beside the salmon so it stands up.
2. Dress the lettuce.
3. Place the parcels in the centre of the plate and the dressed lettuce on top of the salmon.
4. Garnish with the caviar and some herb oil.

Irish Smoked Salmon and Crab Parcel, Served with Orange and Caviar

∞∞

Mussel Chowder with Battered Oysters, Crispy Prawns and a Crème de Cassis Dressing

∞∞

Squab Pigeon Breast, Stuffed Leg, Lamb's Sweetbreads and Truffle Salad

∞∞

Potato and Ham Hock Terrine, Sautéed Mushrooms and Café de Paris Sauce

∞∞

Trio of Sea Bass, Poached with Fennel and Pernod Sauce, Panfried on Crushed Potato and a Peach Glaze, and Deep Fried in a Beer Batter with a Tartar Sauce

∞∞

Seared Shark Fillet with a Mango and Orange Salsa, Served on Nori Seaweed

∞∞

Kir Royale Sorbet

∞∞

Chilled Chocolate Fondant with Cointreau Cream

Potato and Ham Hock Terrine, Sautéed Mushrooms and Café de Paris Sauce (page 107)

Mussel Chowder with Battered Oysters, Crispy Prawns and a Crème de Cassis Dressing

INGREDIENTS (SERVES 8)

200ml mussel chowder (*see p.154*)
8 fresh opened oysters
8 prawns
30g mixed lettuce leaves
100ml beer batter (*see p.154*)

100g plain flour for dusting
30ml Crème de Cassis dressing
(*see p.147*)
1 sheet of spring roll wrapper

METHOD

1. Dust the oysters in the flour and then in the batter. Deep fry till golden and crisp.
2. Cut the sheet of spring roll in strips about 1cm thick and wrap each prawn carefully so that it covers the full length of the prawn. Deep fry the prawns until crispy.

TO SERVE

1. Warm the chowder and serve in a small coffee cup. Place the oysters and prawns beside the cup.
2. Garnish with dressed salad. Drizzle with the Crème de Cassis dressing.

Caramelised Lamb's Sweetbreads, Squab Pigeon Breast and Stuffed Leg with a Truffle Foam

INGREDIENTS (SERVES 4)

90g   lamb's sweetbreads
1/2lt   milk
2   squab pigeons
40g   chicken minced
1 tsp truffle oil
10g   black truffle
120ml truffle foam
30g   salad leaves
1   tomato
30g   cucumber
1   mango
120ml truffle jus

METHOD

1. Remove the legs and the breasts from the pigeons. Remove the thigh bone from the leg leaving the upper bone.

2. Mix the chicken mince with the truffle oil and season with salt and pepper.

3. Lay the 4 legs flat on the work top, with the meat side up. Divide the chicken mix between them. Use cling film to roll each leg into a small cylinder, trying to remove all the air to make it tight. Then roll each leg in a small sheet of tin foil to help them to keep their shape.

4. Bring the milk to the boil in a saucepan and add the sweetbreads. Cook for 7-8 minutes, depending on size. When they are ready, take them out and remove the sinew. Rinse away any milk that is left.

5. Peel and deseed the cucumber, tomato and mango. Chop into small dices, around 3 mm by 3mm.

6. Bring water to the boil in a small pot, add the stuffed pigeon legs and boil them for 3 minutes.
7. Heat the truffle foam without bringing it to the boil.
8. Heat a frying pan and using a little butter, cook the pigeon breasts for about 2-3 minutes on each side. Place on a towel to remove the butter.
9. Dry the pan and put it back on heat. Remove the tin foil and cling film from the legs and fry them quickly in little butter in the pan to give them a nice colour.
10. Dry the pan again and then caramelise the sweetbread in a little butter. Place them on the same towel to remove all the butter from frying.

TO SERVE
1. Combine the salad leaves with the mango, cucumber and tomato.
2. Arrange the salad in a circle around the centre of each plate.
3. Slice the truffle very thin and divide it between the salads.
4. Place the pigeon breast in the centre.
5. Cut away the bottom of the leg to make it flat and then stand it up next to the breast.
6. Divide the sweetbread into 4 and put them around the salad.
7. Foam the sauce using a hand mixer and put a little foam on top of the breast.
8. Drizzle each plate with a circle of the foam.

Potato and Ham Hock Terrine, Sautéed Mushrooms and Café de Paris Sauce (page 104)

INGREDIENTS (MAKES 2KG TERRINE)

4	ham hocks, total weight about 1kg	1kg	large rooster potatoes
1	carrot	100g	butter
100g	leeks	6	slices of Parma ham
50g	shallots	200g	Paris mushrooms
2	bay leaves	40g	mixed lettuce
12	black peppercorns	10ml	Balsamic dressing (see p.147)
		100ml	Café de Paris sauce

METHOD
1. Soak the hocks in cold water overnight to draw out some salt. Discard the water.

→

2. Cover with fresh water and add the carrot, leeks, shallots, bay leaves and peppercorns to the saucepan. Cook for about 3 hours until the meat is falling off the bone.
3. While the hocks are cooking, line a 2kg volume terrine with cling film and then the Parma ham, making sure that the ham covers all the terrine and comes out over the edges so that you can cover the terrine when filled.
4. Bake the potatoes in the oven so that they are ready at the same time as the hocks are almost ready. The hocks and the potatoes should be hot when added to the terrine.
5. Remove the meat from the bone and reserve. Remove the flesh from the potatoes and sieve through a ricer and season, keeping them warm. Season.
6. Starting with the potato, layer the terrine with potato and ham hock, then potato and ham hock and so on until full, then cover with the overlapping Parma ham and cling film. Rest in fridge for 6 hours.

TO SERVE

1. Sauté the mushrooms in the butter and season.
2. Dress the lettuce with some Balsamic dressing and warm the Café de Paris sauce.
3. Slice the terrine about 1cm thick and panfry in some clarified butter until crisp and golden brown.
4. Place the terrine on the sautéed mushrooms, with the dressed lettuce on top.
5. Sauce and serve warm or cold.

Café de Paris sauce

INGREDIENTS

2	shallots, minced		60ml	cream
50g	butter		20g	truffle
30ml	brandy		20g	foie gras
120ml	veal jus (*see p.158*)		2tsp	mixed chopped herbs

METHOD

1. Sauté the shallots in the butter until soft. Add the brandy and flame. Reduce the brandy to almost nothing and add the veal jus.
2. Reduce by half and add the cream. Reduce to coating consistency and then add the rest of the ingredients.
3. Cook for 2-3 minutes and blend. Season.

Oysters with Pickled Cucumber, Lobster Crème Fraiche and Caviar

INGREDIENTS (SERVES 8)

24	oysters		80g	crème fraiche
100ml	white wine vinegar		30ml	lobster fond (*see p. 149*)
100g	sugar		20g	caviar (or a cheaper option)
2	cucumbers			

METHOD

1. Open the oysters and clean off all shell fragments.
2. Combine the sugar and vinegar in a saucepan and bring to the boil – this is the pickling brine (liquid).
3. Peel and deseed the cucumbers, cut into spaghetti lengths and add to the liquid. Allow to cool in the pickling liquid.
4. Add the lobster fond to the crème fraiche and season.

TO SERVE

1. Place some pickled cucumber in each oyster shell, with an oyster on top.
2. Divide the oyster shells between the plates. Spoon some crème fraiche on them and top with some caviar.

Oysters with Pickled
Cucumber, Lobster Crème
Fraiche and Caviar

Cappuccio of Haricot Beans
Served with a
Warm Pavé of Irish Smoked
Salmon Salad

Slow Roasted Venison, Served
with Du Puy Lentils
and a Tea and Brandy Jus

Strawberry Sorbet on
Shortbread Biscuits and
Baileys Anglaise

Lobster and Cod Brandade
with a Carrot Sauce

Roast Stuffed Quail with
Sweetbreads and Chicken,
Served with a Rosemary Jus

Parfait of Tea and Coffee
Anglaise

Cappuccio of Haricot Beans Served with a Warm Pavé of Irish Smoked Salmon Salad

INGREDIENTS (SERVES 8)

300g	haricot beans
1	carrot
1	leek
4	shallots
50g	butter
2tsp	white truffle oil
4	puff pastry sticks (see p.149)
800ml	chicken stock (see p.159)
150ml	cream
120g	smoked salmon
30g	frisée lettuce

METHOD
1. Soak the beans overnight in water and then strain.
2. Roughly chop the vegetables and sweat in the butter until soft. Add the drained haricot beans.
3. Add the stock and cook until beans and vegetables are soft.
4. Purée in a blender. Pass and season.
5. Add the cream and truffle oil to the soup.

TO SERVE
1. Froth some milk as for a cappuccino coffee and place on the top of the soup.
2. Garnish the soup with the puff pastry stick, smoked salmon and dressed lettuce.
3. The soup can be served in a small cappuccino cup (hence the name of the dish)

Slow Roasted Venison, Served with Du Puy Lentils, Tea and Brandy Jus (see page 114)

INGREDIENTS (SERVES 4)

4	venison loins, each of about 90g weight
200g	du Puy lentils, cooked (see p.151)
50ml	chicken stock (see p.159)
100ml	tea and brandy jus

METHOD

1. Reheat the Du Puy lentils in the chicken stock.
2. Seal the venison in butter and roast in the oven at 100°C until the centre of the meat reaches 48°C. Use a thermometer to check this. Alternatively, cook in a hot oven at 200°C for 6-8 minutes.

TO SERVE

1. Slice the venison and place on the Du Puy lentils. Sauce with the tea and brandy jus.

Tea and Brandy Jus

INGREDIENTS

20g	tealeaves
3	shallots, sliced
6	black peppercorns
50g	butter
200ml	game jus (see p.159)
50ml	brandy

METHOD

1. Sauté the shallots, peppercorns and tealeaves in butter.
2. Add the brandy and flame.
3. Add the game jus and reduce by one third.
4. Pass and season.

Strawberry Sorbet on Shortbread Biscuits, with Baileys Anglaise

INGREDIENTS (SERVES 8)

350ml	water	40g	tremoline sugar (optional)
300g	caster sugar	650ml	strawberry purée
90g	glucose	8	shortbread biscuits
1g	sorbet stabiliser (optional)	80ml	Baileys Anglaise
		8	blackberries

METHOD

1. Put all the ingredients except the strawberry purée in a saucepan and boil for just 4 minutes. Remove from the heat and add the strawberry purée.

2. Allow to cool. Finish in an ice cream machine until smooth and creamy.

TO SERVE
1. Put the strawberry sorbet on top of the shortbread biscuits. Serve with the Baileys Anglaise and some blackberries.

Baileys Anglaise

INGREDIENTS

30ml Bailey's Liqueur
100ml vanilla anglaise *(see p.102)*

METHOD
1. Add the Baileys liqueur to the vanilla anglaise.

Shortbread biscuits

INGREDIENTS
300g butter, softened
150g caster sugar
425g flour
1   egg

METHOD
1. Cream the sugar and the butter together and add the egg. Incorporate well and add the flour to form a dough.
2. Allow to rest for 1 hour, then roll out until it is $^1/_2$ cm thick. Cut into circles of about 2cm diameter and place onto a sill mat.
3. Bake in a preheated oven at 180°C for 10-12 minutes till golden brown.
4. Remove onto wire racks and allow to cool.

Brandade of Cod in Brioche Crumbs, Half a Lobster and a Carrot Foam

INGREDIENTS (SERVES 4)

120g	rooster potatoes		200g	lobster
100g	cod		50g	butter
	Flour for dusting		120 ml	carrot white wine sauce
100g	Brioche crumbs (see p.147)			(see p.151)
100ml	Egg wash		1 tsp	chopped parsley
500ml	milk			Seasoning
			1 tsp	chopped garlic

METHOD

1. Cook the potatoes in the oven in their jackets until cooked. Remove flesh.
2. If using live lobster, bring a pot of water to the boil and put in the lobster. Take out after 5 minutes and remove the shell straight away. Clean them under running water.
3. Bring the milk to the boil and poach the cod for 5 minutes. Remove the skin.
4. Press the potatoes through a potato ricer into a metal bowl, add the poached cod and the chopped parsley. Mix well until completely smooth. Season with salt and pepper, garlic and parsley.
5. Use a bit of flour on your hands and mould the mix into 4 small round cakes. Turn them in flour, then dip them in egg wash and finish them by completely covering them with the brioche crumbs. These are brandades.
6. Heat the carrot sauce without bringing it to the boil.
7. Heat up a frying pan, add the butter and then pan-fry the brandades of cod and potato on medium heat for 2 minutes on each side. Put them in a towel to dry.
8. Put a small amount of water in a pot and heat slightly to 65°C. Heat the lobster meat slowly in the water, being careful not to let the water get too hot. Remove after about $1^1/2$ minutes and then put it the towel.

TO SERVE

1. Place one cod brandade in the middle of each plate.
2. Divide the lobster into 4 and put it on the brandades.
3. Add a small amount of milk to the carrot sauce and mix it with a hand mixer- the milk will help it to foam.

MY TIP

Leave the skin on the cod when poaching as it will help the meat to stay together. The cod for brandade is traditionally salted, but you can just use normal cod if desired.

4. Put a spoon of foam on top of the brandade and use the rest to drizzle over the plates.
5. Garnish the plates with baby vegetables, if desired.

Roast Stuffed Quail with Sweetbreads and Chicken, Served with a rosemary Jus

INGREDIENTS (SERVES 8)

4	quails, boned		8	garlic confit
80g	sweetbreads, cooked (see p.160)		8	roasted shallots
			100ml	rosemary jus
50g	chicken mince		1	sweet crépinette
10g	pistachio nuts			

METHOD

1. Dice the sweetbreads and add to the chicken mince, with the pistachio nuts. Season.
2. Stuff the quails with the mince, roll into a cylinder and wrap in crepeinette.
3. Seal the stuffed quails, then roast in the hot oven at 200°C for 10 minutes.

TO SERVE

1. Warm the garlic and shallot confit and use to garnish the plate..
2. Slice the quail and place standing in the centre of the plate. Drizzle with the jus. Each quail serves 2 portions.

Rosemary jus

INGREDIENTS

3	shallots, sliced
6	black peppercorns
50g	butter
2 tsp	rosemary leaves, chopped
100ml	lamb jus (see p.159)

METHOD

1. Sweat the shallots and the peppercorns in the butter till soft. Add the chopped rosemary and the lamb jus and reduce to a coating consistency.
2. Season and pass.

Parfait of Tea and Coffee Anglaise

INGREDIENTS (SERVES 8)

14	egg yolks		20g	Earl Grey tealeaves
4	eggs		100ml	coffee anglaise
280g	caster sugar		8	raspberries
2lt	cream		8	chocolate garnish *(see p.160)*
50g	honey			

METHOD

1. Sabayon the eggs, egg yolks and sugar together until light and fluffy.
2. Whisk the cream to a semi peak and reserve.
3. Diffuse the honey and the tealeaves by heating them no more than 70°C.
4. Fold all the ingredients together and incorporate well.
5. Line a terrine with cling film, add the mix and freeze.

TO SERVE

1. Slice the frozen parfait and serve with some coffee coulis.
2. Garnish with berries and a chocolate garnish.

Coffee anglaise

INGREDIENTS

75ml	milk
25ml	strong black coffee
1	vanilla pod
1	egg yolk
20g	caster sugar

METHOD

1. Boil the milk and coffee together with the vanilla pod and strain.
2. Sabayon the sugar and the yolk together and add the milk. Whisk well and return to the heat to thicken until it coats the back of a wooden spoon.
3. Finish by straining the sauce.

MY TIP
You can also make a coffee anglaise by adding one strong short black coffee to 100ml vanilla anglaise.

Poached Foie Gras Wrapped in Duck Rilette with an Apple Salsa (following page)

Poached Foie Gras Wrapped in Duck Rilette with an Apple Salsa
(page 124)

160g	poached foie gras (see p. 59)	120ml	Apple Schnapps (optional serving)
100g	duck rillette (see p. 15)	4	apple crisps (see p.102)
80g	apple compote (see p. 59)	4	puff pastry sticks (see p.149)
30g	salad leaves	60ml	herb Aioli (see p.148)
1	tomato		Beetroot powder (see p. 149)
1	mango		

INGREDIENTS (SERVES 4)

METHOD

1. Allow the poached foie gras to reach room temperature.
2. Shred the duck rillette into small pieces and spread it on a small sheet of cling film, making sure it is in thin a layer completely covering the base.
3. Place the poached foie gras on top. Roll the cling film tightly around the foie gras so that the rillette is a full circle around the foie gras. Roll it hard to remove all the air. Put the roll into the fridge for a while to let it set.
4. Peel the mango and cut in thin slices, about 1 mm thick. Cut these slices into 1 cm wide strips and cut again diagonally to make small diamonds.
5. Cut the tomato in 4 pieces and deseed them. Carefully removed the skin and then cut the flesh into diamonds, as with the mango.
6. Cut the foie gras into 4 slices and return to the fridge.

TO SERVE

1. Chill 4 small glasses in the freezer for 1 hour.
2. Place the apple compote in a line just off centre on the plate.
3. Divide the mixed leaves on the plate in the same way as the apple compote.
4. Garnish the salad with the diamonds of tomato and mango.
5. Use the puff pasty stick to get the apple crisp to stand up.
6. Put a glass of apple schnapps on each plate. Use glass from freezer (optional).
7. Garnish the each plate with some balsamic reduction and the beetroot powder.
8. Put the foie gras on last just before you serve it.

Poached Foie Gras
Wrapped in Duck Rilette
with an Apple Salsa

Smoked Haddock Soup
with Quail Egg Salad
and Tomato Sauce

Seafood À La Nage
with a Champagne Foam
and Julienne of Vegetables

Champagne Sorbet

Veal Medallions, Creamed
Spinach and Pinenuts,
and Red Wine Jus

Lamb with Potato and Truffle,
Kidney, Sweetbread Ravioli
and a Cinnamon and
Vanilla Jus

Calvados Camembert

White Chocolate Cappuccio
Mousse, with an Earl Gray
Anglaise Froth,
Pistachio Ice Cream and
Biscotti Biscuits

Smoked Haddock Soup with a Quail Egg Salad

INGREDIENTS (SERVES 8)

500g	smoked haddock	500m	cream
100g	leeks and onions (total weight)	100m	fish stock (*see p.159*)
50g	butter	8	quail egg salad, see next page
100m	white wine		

METHOD

1. Peel the onions and clean the leeks. Roughly chop them into small mireapoix and sweat in some butter.
2. Dice the haddock and add to the onions and leeks.

3. Cook for five minutes, add the wine and reduce by half.
4. Add the cream and stock and cook for 20 minutes.
5. Blend in a mixer till smooth. Pass and season.

TO SERVE
1. Serve garnished with the quail egg salad.

Quail Egg Salad and Graffiette Potatoes and a Tomato Sauce

INGREDIENTS (SERVES 4)

16	quail eggs	30ml	mixed lettuce leaves
1	large rooster potato	5ml	balsamic dressing (see p. 147)
80ml	tomato sauce		

METHOD
1. Place the eggs into boiling water for three minutes. Remove to cold water to stop the cooking process. Peel.
2. Peel the potatoes. Put the serrated blade on the mandaline and set the blade as thin as possible. Slice the potato and turn the potato 45° angle before slicing the second time. Each time you slice, turn the potato backwards and forwards so that when sliced, they resemble nets.
3. Deep fry the potatoes at 160°C till golden brown.

TO SERVE
1. Warm the tomato sauce.
2. Cut a little off the bottom of the hardboiled quail eggs so that they will stand up.
3. Place some graffiettes on top, then some dressed lettuce and drizzle with the tomato sauce.

Tomato sauce

INGREDIENTS

3	shallots, sliced	50ml	white wine
50g	butter	100ml	tomato juice
5	black peppercorns	20g	tomato purée

→

Seafood à la Nage*, Champagne Foam with Julienne of Vegetables (following page)

METHOD

1. Sweat the onions in 20g of the butter with the peppercorns till soft. Add the wine and reduce by half.
2. Add the juice and the purée and reduce by half.
3. Finish the sauce with the rest of the butter by whisking it in cold until incorporated. Pass and season.

. . . .

Seafood à la Nage*, Champagne Foam with Julienne of Vegetables
(page 128)

INGREDIENTS (SERVES 8)

720g	shelled seafood, to include prawns, monkfish, salmon and scallops (mix)		50g	leek Julienne
			50g	courgette Julienne
100ml	white wine		50g	butter
200m	champagne foam			Seasoning
50g	carrots Julienne		100ml	lobster fond (see p. 149)

METHOD

1. Poach the fish in the fond and white wine. The fish will take different times to cook so start with the larger pieces, working down to the smaller pieces like prawns and scallops that will not take so long.
2. Blanche and refresh the vegetables separately. Then combine and toss in the butter. Season.

TO SERVE

1. Place the seafood on each plate, foam the sauce and carefully place on top of the fish.
2. Place the vegetables on top.

Champagne Foam

INGREDIENTS

3	shallots, sliced		150ml	cream
6	black peppercorns		100ml	champagne
70g	butter			

→ * à la nage means to swim

METHOD

1. Sweat the onion and peppercorns in 50g of the butter. Add champagne and reduce by half or to a syrup consistency.
2. Add the cream and reduce by half.
3. Finish the sauce with the rest of the butter by whisking it in cold until incorporated. Pass and season.
4. Whisk to foam. Add 20ml of fresh milk at this stage to help foam the sauce.

• •

Champagne Sorbet

INGREDIENTS (SERVES 8)

175g caster sugar	100ml champagne
150ml water	3g sorbet stabilizer (optional)

METHOD

1. Combine all the ingredients in a saucepan and bring to the boil for 3 minutes.
2. Allow to cool. Finish in an ice cream machine and freeze.

• •

Veal Medallions, Served with Creamed Spinach and Pinenuts and Red Wine Jus

INGREDIENTS (SERVES 8)

200g spinach	8	medallions of veal, each 90g in weight
10g pinenuts		
100m cream	50g	butter
100ml red wine jus		Oil for frying

METHOD

1. Wilt the spinach in the butter. Add cream and reduce by half to a sauce consistency. Toast the pine nuts and add to the spinach. Season.
2. Seal the veal medallions for about 2 minutes on each side in oil. This will be medium, cook 2 more minutes for well done.

MY TIP
This dish is very simple yet full of flavour.

TO SERVE

1. Divide the spinach between the plates. Sit a veal medallion on top and sauce with the red wine jus.

Red Wine Jus

INGREDIENTS

50g	butter		150g	veal jus (*see p.158*)
3	shallots, sliced		50ml	red wine
6	black peppercorns			

METHOD

1. Sweat the shallots and peppercorns in the butter.
2. Add the wine and reduce by two-thirds.
3. Add the veal jus and reduce by half. Season and pass.

• •

Lamb Loin with Potatoe and Truffle Crépinette, Kidney and Sweetbread Ravioli with a Cinnamon and Vanilla Jus,

INGREDIENTS (SERVES 4)

200g	lamb loin		4	lamb's kidneys
150g	small rooster potato		120ml	cinnamon and vanilla jus
100 ml	confit oil			(*see p.152*)
1	piece of crépinette			Egg wash
5g	black truffle		4	baby turnips
50ml	olive oil		4	baby carrots
50g	butter		4	baby asparagus
8	sheets of wonton wrapper			
60g	lamb's sweetbreads			

METHOD

1. Slice the potato thinly on the mandaline (page 165). Heat the confit oil to 70°C and cook the potatoes, without colouring, in the oil until soft. Remove from the oil and put them on a towel to dry away all the oil.

→

2. Slice the truffle very thinly. Remove all fat and sinew from the lamb. Cut the loin into 4 small portions, each 50 g.

3. Lay out the crépinette in a thin layer on the worktop. Put 1 slice of potato on the crépinette, then a piece of the lamb loin, a slice of truffle and finish with another slice of potato. Roll the parcel in the crépinette to help it to hold together. Repeat three more times.

4. Cook the lamb's sweetbreads in milk for 7-8 minutes depending on size. Take out and rinse away the milk.

5. Place 4 sheets of the wonton pastry on the worktop. Divide the sweetbreads into 4 and put in the centre of each sheet. Egg wash around them and put another sheet on top. Try to remove all air pockets and then make sure to seal off all the edges carefully. Using a small ring, cut the raviolis into circles.

6. Bring a pot of water to the boil. Heat a frying pan and add the oil and butter. Seal off the lamb loin parcels and the kidneys, then cook in the oven at 180°C for about 4-5 minutes. Remove from the oven and let them rest on a towel.

TO SERVE

1. Heat up the cinnamon and vanilla jus. Heat the baby vegetables in a saucepan with a little water and butter. Cook the raviolis for about 3 minutes and then let them dry on a towel.

2. Trim off the ends of the lamb parcels and put in the center of each plate. Cut ends off kidneys and put one on each plate.

3. Add the sweetbread raviolis and drizzle each plate with the jus. Garnish with the baby vegetables.

MY TIP

To make the cinnamon and vanilla jus, simply add 1 cinnamon stick to the recipe for vanilla jus on page 152

• •

Cambembert (following page)

INGREDIENTS (SERVES 4)

160g	camembert	100g	pistachio nuts
4 slices	banana bread (*see p.41*)	20ml	olive oil

METHOD

1. Blend olive oil and chopped pistachio nuts together.
2. Serve with slices of banana bread.

Cambembert
(page 132)

White Chocolate Cappuccio Mousse, Served with an Earl Grey Anglaise Froth, Pistachio Ice Cream and Biscotti Biscuits

30ml	strong black coffee		1lt	cream
500g	white chocolate		4	scoops of pistachio ice cream
4	eggs		8	biscotti biscuits
6cl	grand marnier liqueur		100ml	Earl Grey Anglaise
5cl	milk		8	blackberries
4	leaves of gelatine		8	strawberries
140g	caster sugar		8	pineapple crisps (see p.102)

(see p.102)

Baltic Ocean Sea Perch with a Lobster Salad and a Blood Orange Dressing (following page)

Baltic Ocean Sea Perch with a Lobster Salad and a Blood Orange Dressing (page 136)

INGREDIENTS (SERVES 4)

4	sea perch fillets, each about 90g in weight	50g	butter
4	lobster claws	10ml	basil oil (see p.148)
4	slices of black truffles	80ml	blood orange dressing

METHOD

1. Remove all the scales and pin bones from the sea perch. Panfry in some butter skin side down for about 2 minutes till crisp. Turn over to finish for about 1 minute.
2. Warm the claws in some butter.

TO SERVE

1. Dress the lettuce leaves with some blood orange dressing and the sliced truffle.
2. Place the leaves on the plate, with the lobster claw and the sea perch.
3. Dress with the rest of the dressing and drizzle with the basil oil.

Blood orange dressing

INGREDIENTS

100ml	blood orange juice	1	egg yolk
50ml	white wine vinegar	100ml	olive oil
1tsp	mustard		

METHOD

1. Place the blood orange juice, white wine vinegar, mustard and egg yolk in a blender and mix till smooth.
2. Add the olive oil very slowly till it is all incorporated and creamy.
3. Pass and season.

Baltic Ocean Sea Perch
with a Lobster Salad
and
Blood Orange Dressing

Cream of Jerusalem Artichoke
Soup

Sautéed Scallops with
Battered Frogs Legs,
Cauliflower Cream and a
Bouillabaisse Dressing

Guinness Sorbet

Roasted Squab Pigeon with
Salferino of Vegetables,
Potato Roesti
and Star Anaise Glaze

Panfried Sea Bream with
Turned Roast Potatoes,
Paris Mushrooms
and a Chive and Coriander
Crème Fraiche

A Selection of Irish Cheeses

Banana Soufflé with
Almond Ice Cream and
Chocolate Sauce

Cream of Jerusalem Artichoke soup

INGREDIENTS (SERVES 8)

500g	Jerusalem artichokes	150g	small mireapoix vegetable
100m	white wine	300ml	cream
200m	chicken or vegetable stock	100g	butter
	(see pgs.158-159)	30g	frisée lettuce
		4	soup sticks (see p.149)

METHOD

1. Clean and peel the artichokes. Chop to the same size as the mireapoix.
2. Sweat the artichokes and mireapoix of vegetables in the butter until softened. Add the wine and reduce till it starts to lightly caramelise.
3. Add the stock and simmer until the vegetables are very soft. Add the cream and reduce slowly for about 20 minutes.
4. Purée in a blender until very smooth. Pass and season.

TO SERVE

1. Serve the soup in a soup cup or bowl, with the soup sticks on the side.

• •

Sautéed Scallops with Battered Frogs Legs and Cauliflower Cream, with a Bouillabaisse Dressing (following page)

INGREDIENTS (SERVES 4)

8	scallops	125ml	cauliflower cream
8	frogs legs	60ml	bouillabaisse dressing (see p.81)
50g	butter	10ml	Balsamic reduction (see p.147)
100ml	batter (see p.154)	8	asparagus tips
	Flour for dusting		Asian marinade

METHOD

1. Clean the scallops and remove and discard the roe. Dry them slightly with a towel.
2. Clean the frog's legs and carefully remove one of the bones. Fold the meat over the remaining bone so that the remaining bone is clean from meat.
3. Place the legs in the Asian marinade for 12 hours.

4. Put the frog's legs into a small bowl with flour, making sure they are covered in flour.
5. Heat the asparagus tips in little water and butter. Heat the cauliflower cream.
6. Cover the frog's legs in the batter and deep-fry them for 3 minutes.
7. Heat a non-stick frying pan and seal off the scallops in the butter for 30 seconds on each side. Put them on a towel to take away the fat.

TO SERVE
1. Dress each plate with a line of the bouillabaisse dressing and 4 dots of balsamic reduction.
2. Use 2 spoons to make 4 small quennel of the cauliflower cream, putting one quellel on each plate.
3. Add 2 scallops and 2 frog's legs to each plate, along with 2 asparagus tips.

Cauliflower cream

INGREDIENTS

1	cauliflower
	milk to cover

METHOD

1. Break the cauliflower into florets and cover with the milk to keep it white. Boil until completely soft.
2. Strain and blend till completely smooth, then pass through a sieve or tamis.
3. Place in a cloth and allow the excess liquid to drain away. Season.

Asian marinade

INGREDIENTS

100ml	soya sauce	5g	fresh ginger
100ml	mirin	5g	fresh garlic
50g	sweet chilli sauce		

METHOD

1. Blend all the ingredients together and pass.

• •

Guinness Sorbet

INGREDIENTS (SERVES 8)

175g	caster sugar
100ml	water
150ml	Guinness
3g	sorbet stabilizer (optional)

METHOD

1. Combine all the ingredients in a saucepan and bring to the boil for 3minutes. Allow to cool.
2. Finish in an ice cream machine. Freeze.

Roasted Squab Pigeon with Salferino of Vegetables, Potato Roesti and Star Anaise Glaze

INGREDIENTS (SERVES 8)

4	squab pigeons
200g	potatoes, peeled
50g	butter
50g	Parisienne carrots
50g	Parisienne turnip
50g	Parisienne celeriac
50g	Parisienne courgettes
10g	pesto
100ml	Star Anise glaze (*see p.154*)
	Seasoning
	Oil for Frying

METHOD

1. Boil the potatoes in salted water for five to seven minutes to activate the starch in the potato. Remove and dry.
2. Grate them while still hot. Season.
3. Pack into a small mould ring about 4 cm in diameter or a blini pan and fry on both sides in oil until golden brown. The starch will help them stick together.
4. Roast the pigeons on the bone in the oven at 220°C for 8-9 minutes.
5. Blanch the vegetables separately and refresh in cold water to stop the cooking process.

$\longrightarrow$

Panfried Sea Bream with Turned Roast Potatoes, Paris Mushrooms and a Chive and Coriander Crème Fraiche (following page)

1. Remove the breasts and the legs from the roast pigeons and place on top of the Roesti.
2. Reheat the vegetables in some butter and serve around the Roesti.
3. Sauce with the Star Anise glaze.

• •

Panfried Sea Bream with Turned Roast Potatoes, Paris Mushrooms and a Chive and Coriander Crème Fraiche (page 142)

INGREDIENTS (SERVES 4)

4	sea bream filets, each about 90g in weight
8	turned baby potatoes
8	Paris mushrooms
20ml	olive oil
20ml	Balsamic vinegar
1tsp	chives, chopped
1tsp	coriander, chopped
10ml	coriander oil (*see p.148*)
5ml	Balsamic reduction (*see p.147*)
60g	crème fraiche

METHOD

1. Cook the potatoes in boiling salted water until soft. Drain, cool and dry.
2. Remove the caps from the mushrooms and rub with olive oil and the Balsamic vinegar. Roast in the oven at 180°C for four to five minutes.
3. Deep fry the potatoes.
4. Panfry the sea bream in some clarified butter until the skin is crisp – about 3 mins on skin side and 1 minute on the other side to finish.

TO SERVE

1. Add the chopped coriander and chives to the crème fraiche and season.
2. Place the mushroom caps on top of the potato so that they look like mushrooms.
3. Quennel the crème fraiche and serve with the fish and potatoes.
4. Drizzle with the Balsamic reduction and coriander oil.

Banana Soufflé with Caramel Ice Cream and Chocolate Sauce

INGREDIENTS (SERVES 8)

500g	banana purée		4	egg yolks
40g	cornflour		8	egg whites
100g	caster sugar		80ml	chocolate sauce

METHOD

1. Heat the banana purée.
2. Combine the cornflour with a little water and mix well. Add to the banana purée

and stir over a gently heat until it thickens like crème patissiere. Allow to cool down.

3. Add the egg yolks and mix well.
4. Whisk the egg whites and sugar to a stiff meringue. Fold everything together.
5. Line individual soufflé moulds with butter and sugar, divide the mix between them, filling them up to the top.
6. Cook at 180°C for 20 minutes.

Caramel Ice Cream

INGREDIENTS

3	egg yolks	50g	sugar
20g	caster sugar	25g	water
200ml	milk	35g	butter
		120ml	cream

METHOD

1. Bring the milk to the boil.
2. Whisk the yolks and 100g sugar together until fluffy and pale. Add milk to this and whisk well.
3. Return to the heat and cook like vanilla anglaise. Be careful not to scramble the eggs.
4. Combine the water and 300g sugar and bring to a dark caramel.
5. Add the cream being careful that it does not splash.
6. Add the butter and whisk until sauce-like consistency. Allow to cool and add to the anglaise.
5. Finish in ice cream machine.

TO SERVE

Serve the Souffle directly from the oven with icecream and chocolate sauce.

Chocolate Sauce

INGREDIENTS

60g	dark chocolate	20g	butter
40ml	cream	5ml	cointreau

METHOD

Melt all the ingredients together over a bain marie (page 163) and mix well. Serve hot or cold.

Bread (page 157)

Pastry cream

INGREDIENTS

500ml milk
2   vanilla podsSS
5   egg yolks
100g   sugar
25g   corn flour
60g   plain flour

METHOD

1. Put the vanilla pods in the milk and bring to the boil.
2. Sabayon the sugar and the egg yolks together.
3. Remove the vanilla pods from the milk and add it to the sabayon mix.
4. Fold in the corn flour and plain flour and pour into a clean pot. Gently heat the mix until it starts to thicken.
5. Remove from the heat and pass until smooth, creamy and thick.

Brioche bread

INGREDIENTS

500g   flour
250ml milk
20g   yeast
2   eggs
6g   sea salt, ground
30g   sugar
150g   butter

METHOD

1. Warm the milk to about 37°C and whisk in the yeast. If the milk is overheated, it will kill the yeast and the bread will not rise.
2. Add the eggs, sugar and the salt to the milk and incorporate. Add the sieved flour and form a dough.
3. Cover with cling film and allow to rest and rise for 40 minutes. Knock back.
4. Place in a 2lt terrine to half full and leave to rise. When it has risen to the top of the terrine, cook in a preheated oven at 200°C for about 30 minutes.

Balsamic reduction

METHOD

Pour 1lt of vinegar into a pot and reduce until the vinegar thickens to the consistency of honey. It should reduce to about 100ml.

Balsamic Dressing / Creme de Casis

INGREDIENTS

20ml   Balsamic vinegar
1tsp   Dijon mustard
1   egg yolk
100ml olive oil
       Seasoning

METHOD

1. Blend the vinegar, mustard and the egg yolk on a medium setting. Add the oil slowly until incorporated and creamy.
2. Pass and season.
N.B. For Creme de Casis dressing replace Balsamic with Casis.

Herb aioli

INGREDIENTS
3   egg yolks
2 tsp   Dijon mustard
1   clove of garlic, crushed
50ml   sherry vinegar
300ml   olive oil
2tsp   chopped herbs

METHOD
1. Blend the egg yolks, mustard, garlic and sherry vinegar together and add the oil slowly to form a mayonnaise.
2. Add the herbs and season.

Herb oil

INGREDIENTS
20g   parsley
20g   chervil
20g   coriander
20g   basil
10g   thyme
100g   olive oil

METHOD
1. Blend all the ingredients in a blender and pass through a fine strainer.

Beetroot oil

INGREDIENTS
50g   cooked beetroot
100ml olive oil
10ml   vinegar, white wine or sherry

METHOD
Blend everything in a blender and pass through a fine strainer.

Basil Oil

INGREDIENTS
200g   basil leaves
500ml olive oil

Coriander Oil

INGREDIENTS
200g   coriander leaves
500ml olive oil

Parsley Oil

INGREDIENTS
200g   parsley
500ml olive oil

METHOD (FOR ALL THE OILS)
1. First wash and dry the leaves and blend in a blender the olive oil.
2. After, place in a muslin cloth and allow the oil to dip through the cloth.

100g   fresh herbs
3lt   water

METHOD

1. Cut the vegetables into mireapoix and sweat everything in the butter so it starts to soften.
2. Add the rest of the ingredients to the vegetables and add the water.
3. Simmer the stock for 1 hour and strain well.

Grouse/ Duck/ Pheasant/ Venison/ Rabbit/ Lamb stock

INGREDIENTS

500g   game bones
50g   butter
200g   mireapoix
200ml red wine
2lt   chicken stock or water
10g   thyme
12   peppercorns
2   bay leaves

METHOD

1. Roast the bones till golden brown and put in a large pot. Deglaze the pan with the red wine and add to the pot.
2. Add everything else and cover with the stock or the water.
3. Simmer for 3-4 hours and skim all the time. Strain and place back onto the stove.
4. Reduce the stock by half or reduce further for a thicker, richer jus.

Fish stock

INGREDIENTS

1kg   white fish bones
50g   shallots
50g   butter
200g   white wine
200g   mireapoix
30g   mushrooms
20g   fresh herbs
50g   fennel
1.5lt water

METHOD

1. Sweat the vegetables in the butter with the bones. Add the wine and reduce by half.
2. Add the water and simmer for 20-30 minutes, strain and reduce by half.

Chicken stock

INGREDIENTS

2kg   chicken bones
12   peppercorns
50g   thyme
200g   mireapoix
50g   butter
3lt   water

METHOD

1. Remove as much fat and skin from the chicken bones. Combine all the ingredients and simmer for 4-6 hours.
2. Skim frequently while simmering. Strain and reduce by half.

Prawn oil

INGREDIENTS
200g   prawn shells
50g   carrots
50g   leeks
2   shallots
6   peppercorns
1   bay leaf
300ml olive oil

METHOD
1. Roast the shells and the vegetables in the oven until the shells turn colour and start to release their fish odour.
2. Put in a pot and add the oil. Heat the contents to about 60°C for two hours. Do not boil as this will discolour the oil.
3. Strain through a cloth and add 2-3 threads of saffron. Allow to cool.

Parmesan crisps

METHOD
1. Grate Parmesan cheese and arrange into the shape you want on sill mat.
2. Cook in a preheated oven at 200°C for 2 minutes, until the cheese is melted and starting to take colour.
3. Remove from oven and take off tray. If you want to shape them, bend them round a rolling pin while they are still hot.

Chocolate garnish

INGREDIENTS
150g   white chocolate
150g   dark chocolate

METHOD
1. Melt the white chocolate over a bain Marie until smooth. Use a palette knife to spread it thinly on a sill mat. Use a fork or something similar to create a pattern in the chocolate and then put it in the fridge until it gets hard.
2. Melt the dark chocolate without getting it too hot. Quickly pour the dark chocolate over the white chocolate, using a palette knife to get the layer as thin as possible.
3. Return to the fridge to let it go hard again.
4. Remove from the fridge and cut into the shapes you want.
5. These chocolate garnishes will last for several days in the fridge if stored in a container.

Cooking lobsters

Cook the lobsters in boiling water for 6 minutes and then take out. Remove the shells while they are still hot.

Cooking sweetbreads

Bring some milk to the boil and add the sweetbreads. Cook lamb sweetbreads for 8 minutes and veal sweetbreads for 12 minutes. Remove from milk and refresh. At this stage, remove as much membrane as possible.

Beetroot Dressing

INGREDIENTS
100g   cooked beetroots
100ml olive oil
10g   Dijon mustard
20ml   white wine vinegar
       Seasoning

METHOD
Combine all the ingredients in a blender until smooth.
Pass and season.

Mango and Orange salsa

INGREDIENTS
1   orange
1   mango
1   tomato
20g   brunoise of cucumber
50ml   olive oil
5g   Dijon mustard
         Seasoning

METHOD
1.   Skin and deseed the tomato. Peel the mango.
2.   Peel the orange and segment it, keeping the juice.
3.   Brunoise all the fruit.
4.   Mix all the ingredients together and season to taste.

Irish Whiskey Sauce

INGREDIENTS
50g   butter
3   shallots, sliced
4   black peppercorns
150ml lamb jus (see p.159)
50ml   cream (optional)
50ml   Irish whiskey

METHOD
1.   Sweat the shallots and peppercorns in butter until the shallots are soft.
2.   Add the whiskey and flame.
3.   Reduce by half and add the lamb jus and cream. Reduce to coating consistency and pass.   Season.

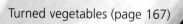
Turned vegetables (page 167)

Glossary of Cooking Terms, Ingredients and Equipment

Al dente: A term used to describe vegetables, such as carrots, that have been cooked so that there is still some bite left in them.

À la nage: A cooking process used to poach fish or vegetables in a stock e.g. Lobster à la nage – cooking lobster in a lobster stock.

Bain Marie: A method in which food can either be cooked or kept warm, by using water as a conductor of heat.

Blind baking: A way of ensuring that the pastry doesn't collapse into a mould during baking. Simply cover the pastry-lined mould with greaseproof paper and fill with rice, lentils or dried beans.

Brunoise: A term used in the cutting of vegetables. A minute dice of vegetables, it is achieved by cutting the vegetables into thin strips and then cutting diagonally across the strips again.

Clarified butter: Butter that has been melted and allowed to separate. The liquid part of the butter is carefully removed from the solids that have settled on the bottom. This liquid part of the butter is then used in cooking because it has a higher flash point and does not burn as quickly as normal butter.

Coating consistency: To cook a sauce until it is sufficiently thick to stick to the food or plate like honey.

Colour: This is the term used when the flesh of the meat or fish, having been placed on a hot pan with some oil or butter, starts to caramelise and become a golden brown colour on the outside without being cooked on the inside.

Compote/chutney: Words used to describe the consistency of a product.
Compote of apple is like stewed apples that have been cooked with other ingredients. Chutney is like a jam.

Crépinette: This is the lining of a pig's stomach. It comes in thin sheets of marble and is pure fat. It is used to wrap around meat to hold it together when cooking, but will melt away during the cooking process leaving the meat in the required shape.

Deglaze: This involves using the caramelised particles left in the baking tray on which meat or bones for a stock have been baked in the oven. To remove these (they are full of flavour), pour wine or water unto the hot tray and scrape them with a wooden spoon. This is to deglaze.

Drizzle: This describes a way of pouring/trickling a small quantity of sauce onto a plate, generally for decorative purposes.

Egg wash: A mixture of eggs and milk, generally one egg to every 100ml of milk. It has a number of uses.

Farce: A meat or fish that has been puréed, blended with some cream and passed through a sieve or tamis to achieve a smooth, mousse-like consistency. It is generally used to stuff or spread on to a product or dish, such as sole paupiette.

Flame: This is when you add some spirit, such as brandy, to a pot or pan and it starts to burn and flame. The alcohol burns away leaving the flavour of the spirit.

Foam: A method used for sauces or soups. When the finished sauce or soup is passed and ready to serve, whisk with a bar mix or hand whisk until a foam forms on top like a cappuccino. Skim off the foam and use – it has all the flavour of the sauce but is much lighter.

Foie Gras: Goose or duck liver that has been grossly enlarged by over feeding or force-feeding the bird.

Gelatine: A colourless, odourless substance extracted from the bones and cartilage of animals, it is available in powder or leaves and used to make jellies and for setting cold liquids or mousses. It has to be soaked in some cold water first.

Glaze: This is a jus that has been reduced by half its volume so that it becomes thick and syrupy.

Glucose: The purist of sugar, it is found naturally in humans, fruit and vegetables. Commercially, it is made by heating together starch and some amino acids.

Gnocchi: Small dumplings made of flour, potato or choux pastry.

Julienne: A term used in the cutting of vegetables, it describes those that have been cut into thin strips about 2.5cm long to look like very thin matches.

Jus: A French word that means juice. This is a stock that has been reduced by half or to a coating consistency. The English call this gravy.

Knock back: A term used in the preparation of a yeast-based dough that has risen like bread. The air is then knocked out of it and the product worked on. This shows that the yeast is fresh and working.

Mandaline: A vegetable slicer that consists of two adjustable steel blades, one plain, one grooved, within a wooden, plastic or steel frame. It is used to slice vegetables with precision.

Mille feuille: The French phrase for a thousand leaves or, in cooking, a thousand layers.

Mireapoix: A term used in the cutting of vegetables. A mireapoix consists of carrots, celery, onion and leeks that have been roughly chopped, for using in the making of soups and stocks. The size of the pieces may vary.

Mirin: A Chinese rice wine, found in Asian supermarkets.

Nori seaweed: A type of Japanese seaweed that comes in paper-like sheets about 12cm by 4cm. It becomes pliable when wet.

Panache: A French word used to describe a mixture of things, such as nuts.

Parisienne: A classic French method of preparing vegetables, using small ball-like objects to prepare them.

Parmetiere: Another French word for describing a particular way of cutting vegetables, namely in dices of about 3mm by 3mm.

Pass: Like to strain, this is done through a sieve, a strainer or a tamis, to remove any lumps so the texture will become smooth.

Pave: Meaning a slab or block, the word is used for dishes in that shape.

Paysanne: Another classic French method of preparing a selection of vegetables to that they are cut into even-sized sticks or lengths and then across into thin slices.

Pectin: The natural compound in fruit that allows a jam to set. It can also be bought in powder form.

Petit fours: The small, bite-sized chocolates or pastries usually served with tea or coffee at the end of the meal.

Pithivier: A large, round, puff pastry tart with scalloped edges, filled with something. It is traditionally served in the French town of the same name.

Polenta: Corn meal porridge from northern Italy that is traditionally made with water in a large copper pot. Maize is also used but takes longer to cook.

Purée: This describes a product (e.g. carrots, fruit) cooked until very soft then blended or passed to become very smooth in texture.

Quenelle: A farce or purée that is moulded into the shape of a sausage or egg, using two spoons.

Refresh: A way to cool something down quickly by putting into iced water to stop the cooking process. Vegetables are often cooked then refreshed and heated up later in some hot water or butter.

Ricer: Like a large garlic press in shape, this piece of equipment allows you to pass potato through it so that it comes out looking like rice - hence its name.

Roux: Process by which equal quantities of flour and butter are cooked together to form a dough-like mix. Used for thickening sauces and soups.

Sabayon: Used all the time in pastry cooking, this is the method used to whisk eggs or egg yolks with sugar until light and fluffy and pale in colour, while also increasing the volume.

Salfernio: Parisienne of vegetables that have been cooked and bound with a stock or sauce e.g. the relevant recipe in this book is bound with a pesto sauce. The term salfernio can also be applied to meat and game e.g. Salfernio of pigeon leg.

Sauté: A cooking method when meat, fish or vegetables have been tossed and cooked very quickly until brown in a very hot pan with some butter or oil in it.

Seal: The term used when the meat is placed on a hot pan with some oil or butter to retain all the juices in the meat while cooking.

Smoking machine: This is basically a steel box (the one I use is the size of a shoe box) that can be completely enclosed to seal in the smoke and the heat. It comprises a tray to hold the wood chips, a wire rack on which to place whatever you want to smoke, a lid to seal it and a handle. The time the item takes to smoke depends on what you are smoking.

Sill mat: In the shape and texture of a rubber mat, it is used in baking to prevent the item being cooked from sticking to the mat during cooking.

Sorbet stabilizer: A powder used by professionals when making sorbets to help the sorbet hold together and not become too hard when frozen.

Strain: This means to pass a liquid such as soup or sauce through a sieve to remove any lumps so that it becomes smooth and creamy in texture.

Sweat: To cook in some butter until soft, without colouring.

Tamis: A wooden or steel circle with fine wire mesh through which a solid such as carrot purée is passed to remove any lumps.

Tremoline sugar: Pure sugar in its raw form, it is used in sorbets and ice cream recipes. It is very similar to glucose sugar.

Trimmings: The leftovers of a product that has been used for another purpose in the dish e.g. the tomato petals that are made from the flesh, the skin and seeds having been kept to make stock.

Turned potato: A term used when a potato or vegetable has been cut into a barrel shape with seven sides, like a hexagon. (see page 162)

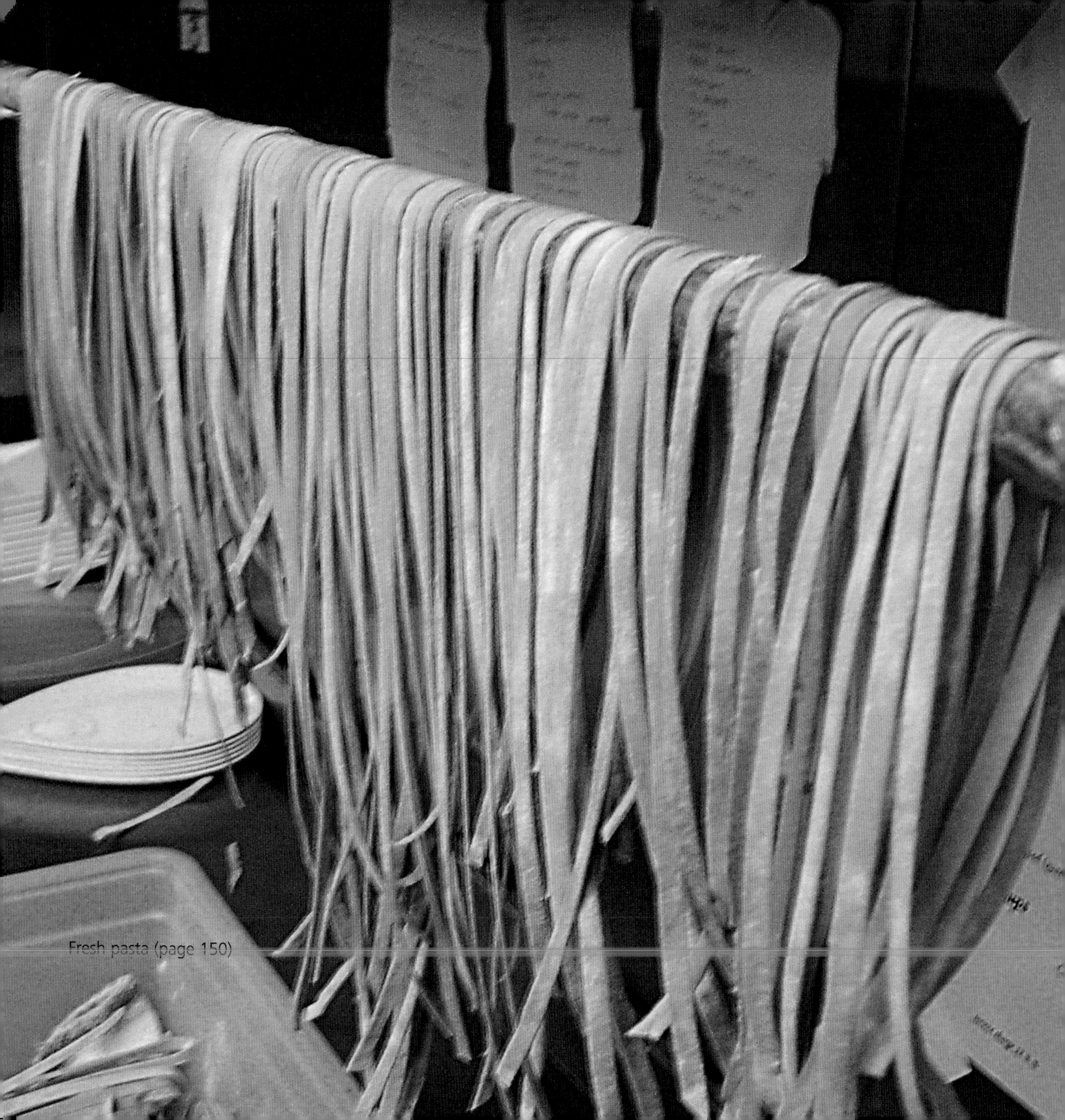

Fresh pasta (page 150)

Index of Menus and Recipes

Acknowledgements

Firstly, my team in the kitchen at Locks without whom my job would be so much harder. All too often these are the people who are forgotten, but in truth they can make both the chef and the restaurant successful. Let's face it, the chef can not do everything. My thanks to Peter Murray, Dominique Majecki and Adell, for their loyalty and passion. Your dedication and friendship mean a lot to me.

Sylvain Costrowa, my sous chef in the kitchen. He has been with me since the beginning of September 2003 and I cannot imagine being without him. His professional and passionate approach to the job is wonderful. A true gentleman, he runs the kitchen with complete control and never forgets that quality and consistency are of the greatest importance. Whatever accolades I earn, Sylvain will be just as much in credit. Did I mention that he is also a very good friend? He can also cook, which helps, but being French he would tell you that that was a given.

Jonas Akerman. I have known Jonas from the time I spent in Sweden. He is an excellent young chef and friend/brother to me. Jonas has worked with me for almost three years and he never fails to amaze me with his passion for learning the art of cooking. His dedication and loyalty to the restaurant and to me are unbelievable. The work that he put into this book in his own time and with no financial gain speaks volumes about his character. It would be a huge loss of both friendship and a great chef if we were not to continue working together. Words are not enough to say thank you. So cheers, mate.

Claire Douglas and Jamie Douglas, the owners of Locks restaurant, without whose financial and personal support this book would not have been possible. They also like my cooking which is a big help as it gives me the freedom to create the dishes featured here.

Judith Elmes, the editor at Ashfield Press. Without her professional approach and ideas this book would have taken forever. Her approach to the work made her an absolute dream to work with. If I were to write another book, Judith would be the first person I would go to.

Susan Waine, the designer at Ashfield Press. Susan did all the lay out and design for this book. The quality speaks for itself. What a true professional.

Not forgetting John Davey, the commercial brain behind Ashfield Press. Without John, the book would not have got off the ground or out to the shops. I am deeply grateful. Through the ups and downs of getting this book to the public, not once did this team think it could not be done, even when I had given up

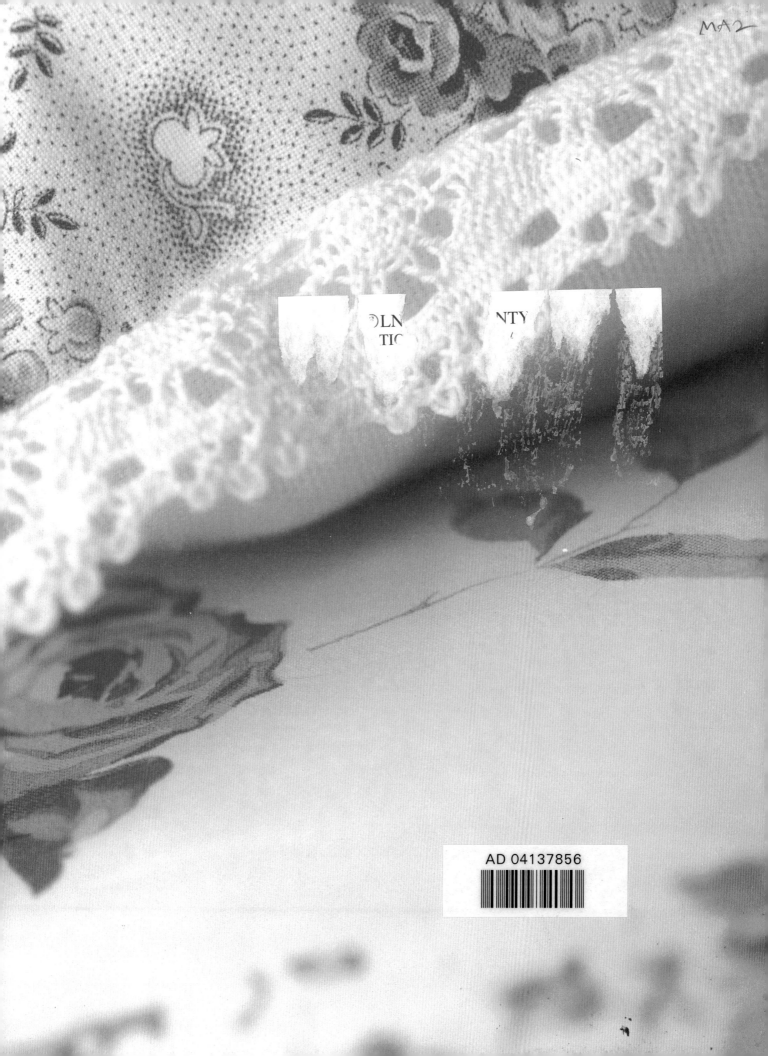

MA2